CONTENTS

1. Foundations of Cost Management.
2. Cost Planning
3. Cost Control
4. Risk Management and Cost
5. Value Engineering
6. Contract Management and Cost
7. Cost Reporting and Communication
8. Sustainability and Cost Management
9. Continuous Improvement in Cost Management
10. Future Trends in Cost Management
11. Conclusion

INTRODUCTION

In the complex landscape of project management, where success hinges on myriad factors, one element stands out as indispensable: cost management. It is the linchpin that holds together the intricate web of project planning, execution, and delivery. Welcome to "Mastering Cost Management: Strategies for Effective Project Budgeting and Control," where we embark on a journey to unravel the mysteries and intricacies of cost management in the realm of project execution.

This book is not just about balancing budgets or crunching numbers; it's about understanding the essence of cost management and harnessing its power to steer projects towards triumph. From historical roots to modern methodologies, from fundamental principles to advanced techniques, we delve deep into every facet of cost management to equip you with the knowledge and tools needed to navigate the challenges of project cost control effectively.

So why does mastering cost management matter? Because it's the difference between project success and failure, between meeting stakeholders' expectations and falling short, between achieving profitability and incurring losses. Whether you're a seasoned project manager, a budding professional, or a curious student, the insights shared in this book will empower you to take charge of costs, mitigate risks, and drive projects towards triumphant fruition.

What is Cost Management

Cost management is the systematic process of planning,

estimating, budgeting, controlling, and analysing costs throughout the project lifecycle. It encompasses a wide array of activities aimed at ensuring that projects are completed within budgetary constraints while meeting quality standards and stakeholder expectations. At its core, cost management involves striking a delicate balance between project requirements, available resources, and financial constraints to achieve optimal outcomes. It involves not only the identification and quantification of costs but also the implementation of strategies to optimize resource utilization and minimize expenditure. In essence, cost management serves as a guiding beacon, illuminating the path towards project success amidst the turbulent seas of uncertainty and complexity.

Evolution of Cost Management

The evolution of cost management is a rich tapestry woven through the annals of history, reflecting the changing landscape of project execution and management practices. From ancient civilizations to the modern era, the concept of managing costs has been integral to the success of endeavours spanning construction, engineering, commerce, and beyond.

In ancient times, rudimentary forms of cost management emerged as civilizations endeavoured to allocate resources efficiently for monumental construction projects such as the pyramids of Egypt or the Great Wall of China. Records indicate early attempts to estimate material and labour costs, albeit in simple forms compared to modern methodologies.

The industrial revolution marked a significant milestone in the evolution of cost management, as mass production and mechanization necessitated more structured approaches to cost estimation and control. The advent of accounting principles and managerial practices laid the groundwork for modern cost management techniques, with pioneers like Frederick Winslow Taylor and Henry Ford championing scientific methods for efficiency and cost reduction.

The 20th century witnessed a rapid proliferation of cost management methodologies, spurred by advancements in technology, globalization, and the emergence of project management as a distinct discipline. Techniques such as Activity-Based Costing (ABC), Earned Value Management (EVM), and Total Cost Management (TCM) gained prominence, offering sophisticated tools for project cost estimation, monitoring, and control.

In the contemporary era, cost management continues to evolve in response to dynamic market forces, regulatory changes, and technological innovations. Concepts such as life cycle costing, value engineering, and sustainability have gained traction, reflecting a broader understanding of costs beyond traditional financial metrics.

As we embark on this journey to master cost management, it is essential to appreciate its evolutionary trajectory, drawing inspiration from the lessons of the past while embracing the opportunities of the future. By understanding the roots of cost management and the forces that have shaped its development, we can navigate the complexities of modern projects with clarity, confidence, and foresight.

Objectives of the Book

The objectives of "Mastering Cost Management: Strategies for Effective Project Budgeting and Control" are multifaceted, designed to empower readers with the knowledge, skills, and insights necessary to excel in the realm of cost management within project management contexts. As you embark on this enlightening journey, the following objectives serve as guiding beacons, illuminating the path towards mastery:

This book seeks to provide clarity on the purpose and scope of cost management within the broader context of project management. By elucidating key concepts, principles, and methodologies, readers gain a comprehensive understanding of how cost management contributes to project success.

Through practical examples, case studies, and exercises, this book equips readers with a toolkit of cost management techniques and strategies. From cost estimation and budgeting to variance analysis and risk mitigation, readers learn how to apply these tools effectively in real-world scenarios.

Beyond rote memorization, this book fosters critical thinking and problem-solving skills essential for effective cost management. By engaging with thought-provoking questions and scenarios, readers learn to analyse complex situations, identify challenges, and devise creative solutions.

Cost management transcends traditional boundaries, intersecting with disciplines such as finance, accounting, engineering, and project management. This book bridges these divides, promoting cross-disciplinary understanding and collaboration to enhance project outcomes.

Mastery of cost management is an ongoing journey, requiring a commitment to continuous learning and improvement. This book instils a mindset of lifelong learning, encouraging readers to stay abreast of emerging trends, technologies, and best practices in cost management.

By demystifying complex cost management concepts and providing practical guidance, this book inspires confidence and empowerment in readers. Armed with knowledge and skills, readers are better equipped to navigate the challenges of cost management with resilience and resolve.

Ultimately, the overarching objective of this book is to empower readers to become proficient practitioners of cost management, capable of driving projects towards success through effective budgeting, control, and strategic decision-making. As you delve into the chapters that follow, may these objectives serve as guiding principles on your path towards mastery.

Who is this book for.

"Mastering Cost Management: Strategies for Effective Project

Budgeting and Control" is tailored to meet the needs of a diverse audience spanning various professions, industries, and educational backgrounds. The book caters to individuals and organizations involved in project management, construction, engineering, finance, and related fields. The target audience includes, but is not limited to, the following:

Project Managers: Professionals responsible for overseeing project execution, from initiation to completion, benefit from the comprehensive understanding of cost management principles and practices offered in this book. They learn how to develop and manage project budgets, monitor costs, and make informed decisions to ensure project success.

Cost Estimators and Quantity Surveyors: Individuals involved in estimating project costs, quantifying resources, and preparing budgetary estimates gain valuable insights into advanced cost estimation techniques, risk management strategies, and value engineering principles. They enhance their ability to produce accurate cost estimates and optimize resource utilization.

Construction and Engineering Professionals: Architects, engineers, contractors, and other stakeholders involved in construction and engineering projects benefit from the practical guidance and case studies presented in the book. They learn how to navigate the complexities of cost management in the context of infrastructure development, building construction, and engineering projects.

Finance and Accounting Professionals: Professionals in finance and accounting roles play a crucial role in budgeting, financial analysis, and cost control within organizations. This book equips them with a deeper understanding of cost management principles and methodologies, enabling them to collaborate effectively with project teams and contribute to sound financial decision-making.

Students and Academics: Students pursuing degrees in project management, construction management, engineering, finance, and related disciplines find the book to be a valuable resource for academic learning and professional development. It serves as a comprehensive guide to understanding cost management concepts, theories, and practical applications, preparing students for future careers in their respective fields.

Consultants and Industry Professionals: Consultants, industry analysts, and professionals seeking to enhance their knowledge and expertise in cost management find the book to be a valuable resource for staying abreast of industry trends, best practices, and emerging technologies. They leverage the insights and practical guidance offered in the book to deliver value-added services to clients and organizations.

Why Cost Management Matters

Mastering cost management isn't merely a professional endeavour; it's a strategic imperative with far-reaching implications for project success, organizational performance, and stakeholder satisfaction. Here's why honing your skills in cost management matters:

Project Success and Viability: Effective cost management is foundational to project success. By accurately estimating, budgeting, and controlling costs, project managers ensure that initiatives are completed within resource constraints and meet stakeholders' expectations for quality, scope, and schedule.

Financial Health and Sustainability: Cost management directly impacts an organization's financial health and long-term sustainability. By optimizing resource allocation, minimizing waste, and identifying cost-saving opportunities, organizations enhance profitability, competitiveness, and resilience in dynamic market environments.

Risk Mitigation and Contingency Planning: Cost management serves as a critical tool for risk mitigation and contingency planning. By identifying potential cost risks, assessing their impact, and implementing proactive measures, project teams safeguard against budget overruns, delays, and unforeseen challenges.

Resource Optimization and Efficiency: Efficient resource allocation is at the heart of cost management. By aligning resources with project requirements, organizations maximize productivity, minimize idle time, and optimize the utilization of labour, materials, and equipment, thereby enhancing operational efficiency and profitability.

Stakeholder Confidence and Trust: Transparent and effective cost management fosters stakeholder confidence and trust. By providing accurate cost projections, timely updates, and proactive communication, project teams demonstrate accountability, reliability, and professionalism, fostering positive relationships with clients, investors, and other stakeholders.

Strategic Decision-Making and Value Creation: Cost management enables strategic decision-making and value creation. By evaluating costs in the context of project objectives, organizational goals, and market dynamics, decision-makers can prioritize investments, allocate resources strategically, and maximize value for stakeholders.

Compliance and Governance: Cost management ensures compliance with regulatory requirements, contractual obligations, and internal governance standards. By adhering to established cost control procedures, organizations mitigate legal and financial risks, uphold ethical standards, and safeguard against reputational damage.

Continuous Improvement and Innovation: Mastery of cost management fosters a culture of continuous improvement and innovation. By analysing cost performance, identifying areas for optimization, and embracing emerging technologies and best practices, organizations drive efficiencies, foster innovation, and maintain a competitive edge in the marketplace.

In essence, mastering cost management isn't just about crunching numbers; it's about fostering a mindset of strategic stewardship, value creation, and continuous improvement. By honing your skills in cost management, you empower yourself and your organization to navigate the complexities of project execution with confidence, resilience, and foresight, ultimately driving success, sustainability, and stakeholder satisfaction.

CHAPTER 1: FOUNDATIONS OF COST MANAGEMENT

Understanding Costs

Costs are the cornerstone of any project, serving as the foundation upon which all financial decisions are made. In this section, we delve into the intricacies of costs, examining their definition, classification, and significance in project management.

Definition of Costs in Project Management:

Costs encompass all expenditures incurred in the execution of a project, including labour, materials, equipment, and overhead expenses. They represent the financial resources required to deliver project deliverables within specified constraints.

Understanding the concept of costs is essential for everyone involved, as it forms the basis for budgeting, resource allocation, and decision-making throughout the project lifecycle.

Direct vs. Indirect, Fixed vs. Variable:

Costs can be categorized based on their relationship to project activities and their variability in relation to project output.

Direct costs are directly attributable to a specific project activity or work package, such as labour and materials.

Indirect costs, also known as overhead costs, are not directly tied to a specific activity but contribute to the overall project, such as administrative expenses and utilities.

Costs can also be classified as fixed or variable. Fixed costs remain constant regardless of project output, while variable costs fluctuate based on the volume of project activities.

Different Cost Elements:

Labor costs encompass wages, salaries, and benefits associated with personnel involved in project execution.

Material costs include the expenses incurred for purchasing raw materials, supplies, and equipment necessary for project implementation.

Equipment costs refer to the expenditure associated with renting, leasing, or purchasing machinery, tools, and technology used in project activities.

Overheads comprise indirect costs such as administrative expenses, utilities, rent, and insurance that support project operations but are not directly attributable to specific activities.

Understanding the nuances of costs enables project managers to develop accurate cost estimates, allocate resources efficiently, and monitor project expenditures effectively. By mastering the fundamentals of cost management, project teams can lay a solid foundation for successful project delivery and stakeholder satisfaction.

Cost Terminology and Concepts

Now we delve into the essential terminology and concepts that form the basis of cost management in project environments. Clear understanding of these terms is crucial for effective communication, planning, and control of project costs.

Cost Estimation: Cost estimation involves predicting the expenses associated with project activities based on historical data, expert judgment, and other relevant factors. It provides an initial assessment of the financial resources required to execute the project.

Cost Budgeting: Cost budgeting entails allocating the estimated project costs to specific tasks, work packages, or time periods. It involves the development of a detailed budget plan that outlines how project funds will be allocated and managed throughout the project lifecycle.

Cost Control: Cost control refers to the process of monitoring, measuring, and managing project costs to ensure they remain within the approved budget. It involves tracking actual expenditures, identifying variances from the budget, and implementing corrective actions as necessary to prevent cost overruns.

Cost Baseline:

A cost baseline represents the approved budget for the project, against which actual costs are measured and compared throughout the project lifecycle.

It serves as a benchmark for evaluating project performance, assessing variances, and making informed decisions to keep the project on track financially.

Establishing a cost baseline early in the project ensures alignment with stakeholder expectations, facilitates cost monitoring and control, and enhances accountability for project expenditures.

A **Cost Breakdown Structure (CBS)** is a hierarchical breakdown of project costs by category, element, or resource type. It provides a systematic framework for organizing and tracking project costs, enabling detailed analysis, and reporting.

The **Work Breakdown Structure (WBS)** is a hierarchical decomposition of the project scope into smaller, manageable components or work packages. It serves as the foundation for developing the CBS and allocating costs to specific project activities.

Clear understanding of these fundamental cost terminology and concepts lays the groundwork for effective cost management practices in project environments. By mastering these concepts, project managers can develop comprehensive cost estimates, establish realistic budgets, and implement robust cost control measures to ensure project success.

Cost Estimation Techniques

Cost estimation is a critical aspect of project planning, providing stakeholders with valuable insights into the financial resources required to execute the project successfully. In this section, we explore various techniques used to estimate project costs accurately.

Analogous estimating, also known as top-down estimating, relies on historical data from similar past projects to predict the costs of current projects.

This technique is often used in the early stages of project planning when detailed information is limited. By leveraging historical data, project managers can quickly generate rough cost estimates based on the similarities between the current and past projects.

Parametric estimating involves using statistical relationships between historical data and project parameters (such as size, complexity, or productivity rates) to estimate project costs.

This technique is based on mathematical models or algorithms that quantify the relationship between project characteristics and costs. It is particularly useful for repetitive tasks or activities with well-defined parameters.

Bottom-up estimating involves estimating the costs of individual project components or work packages and aggregating them to develop the overall project cost estimate.

This technique is highly detailed and requires a thorough understanding of the project scope, requirements, and resource needs. It is often used in conjunction with the Work Breakdown

Structure (WBS) to ensure comprehensive coverage of project costs.

Three-point estimating, also known as Program Evaluation and Review Technique (PERT), uses three estimates—optimistic, pessimistic, and most likely—to calculate an expected cost for a project activity.

By incorporating uncertainty and variability into the estimation process, PERT provides a more realistic and probabilistic view of project costs, allowing for better risk assessment and contingency planning.

Each of these cost estimation techniques has its strengths and limitations, and the choice of technique depends on factors such as project complexity, available data, and stakeholder preferences. By leveraging these techniques effectively, project managers can develop accurate and reliable cost estimates that form the basis for sound project planning and decision-making.

Cost Budgeting

Cost budgeting is a critical process in project management that involves allocating the estimated project costs to specific tasks, work packages, or time periods. We will now explore the key concepts and considerations involved in cost budgeting.

Developing project budgets entails translating the estimated project costs into a comprehensive budget plan that outlines the financial resources required for project execution.

Budgets can be developed at various levels of detail, from high-level estimates to detailed budgets for individual tasks or work packages. The level of detail depends on factors such as project complexity, available data, and stakeholder requirements.

While cost estimates provide an initial assessment of project costs, cost budgets represent the approved allocation of funds for specific project activities or deliverables.

Cost budgets are typically developed based on the cost estimates, considering additional factors such as risk management, contingency planning, and resource constraints.

Budget allocation involves distributing the project budget among various tasks, work packages, or cost categories based on their relative importance, priority, and resource requirements.

Resource planning involves identifying the human, material, and financial resources needed to execute the project activities within the allocated budget. It ensures that the project has access to the necessary resources to meet its objectives effectively.

Once the project budget is established, it serves as a baseline against which actual costs are measured and compared throughout the project lifecycle.

Cost control involves monitoring project costs, identifying variances from the budget, and implementing corrective actions as necessary to prevent cost overruns and ensure that the project remains within budgetary constraints.

Cost budgeting is an iterative process that requires collaboration and coordination among project stakeholders, including project managers, sponsors, and team members. By developing comprehensive budget plans and implementing robust cost control measures, project teams can effectively manage project costs and ensure the successful delivery of project objectives within budgetary constraints.

Cost Control Principles

Cost control is a fundamental aspect of project management, ensuring that project costs are managed effectively throughout the project lifecycle. In this section, we explore the principles and strategies underlying cost control practices.

Cost control is essential for ensuring that projects are completed within the approved budgetary constraints while meeting quality standards and stakeholder expectations.

Effective cost control enables project managers to identify

potential cost overruns, mitigate risks, and make informed decisions to keep the project on track financially.

Cost control is often used interchangeably with cost management, but they represent distinct processes within the project management framework.

While cost management encompasses the entire lifecycle of cost-related activities, including estimation, budgeting, and control, cost control specifically focuses on monitoring, measuring, and managing project costs to ensure they remain within the approved budget.

Variance analysis involves comparing actual project performance against the planned baseline to identify deviations from the budget.

Schedule variance (SV) measures the difference between the earned value (EV) and the planned value (PV) of project activities, indicating whether the project is ahead of or behind schedule.

Cost variance (CV) measures the difference between the earned value (EV) and the actual cost (AC) of project activities, indicating whether the project is under or over budget.

Earned Value Management (EVM) is a systematic approach to measuring and tracking project performance against the project baseline.

Key EVM metrics include Planned Value (PV), Earned Value (EV), and Actual Cost (AC), which provide insights into the project's schedule and cost performance.

Performance indices such as Schedule Performance Index (SPI) and Cost Performance Index (CPI) indicate whether the project is meeting, exceeding, or falling short of performance expectations.

Cost control involves implementing corrective actions to address identified variances and deviations from the budget.

Corrective actions may include adjusting project schedules, reallocating resources, revising cost estimates, renegotiating contracts, or implementing efficiency measures to mitigate risks and prevent cost overruns.

By adhering to these cost control principles and leveraging appropriate tools and techniques, project managers can effectively manage project costs, minimize risks, and ensure the successful delivery of project objectives within budgetary constraints.

Earned Value Management (EVM)

Earned Value Management (EVM) is a powerful technique used in project management to measure and track project performance against the planned baseline. In this section, we delve into the principles, metrics, and benefits of EVM.

Earned Value Management (EVM) is a systematic approach that integrates project scope, schedule, and cost to assess project performance objectively.

It provides project managers with a comprehensive set of metrics and indicators to measure progress, identify trends, and forecast future performance.

Planned Value (PV), also known as Budgeted Cost of Work Scheduled (BCWS), represents the authorized budget allocated to scheduled work at a specific point in time.

Earned Value (EV), also known as Budgeted Cost of Work Performed (BCWP), represents the value of work completed and approved according to the project plan.

Actual Cost (AC) also known as Actual Cost of Work Performed (ACWP), represents the total costs incurred for the work performed during a specific time period.

Schedule Performance Index (SPI) measures the efficiency of schedule performance by comparing the earned value (EV) to the planned value (PV). SPI = EV / PV. An SPI greater than 1 indicates ahead of schedule performance, while an SPI less than

1 indicates behind schedule performance.

Cost Performance Index (CPI): CPI measures the efficiency of cost performance by comparing the earned value (EV) to the actual cost (AC). CPI = EV / AC. A CPI greater than 1 indicates cost under-run, while a CPI less than 1 indicates cost over-run.

Benefits of EVM:

•   Objective Performance Measurement: EVM provides objective metrics for measuring project performance, allowing stakeholders to assess progress accurately and make informed decisions.

•   Early Detection of Issues: EVM facilitates early detection of schedule delays, cost overruns, and performance deviations, enabling timely corrective actions to be implemented.

•   Forecasting and Trend Analysis: EVM allows project managers to forecast future performance based on current trends and performance indices, helping to anticipate potential risks and challenges.

•   Improved Communication: EVM enhances communication and transparency among project stakeholders by providing a common language and framework for discussing project performance.

Successful implementation of EVM requires careful planning, stakeholder buy-in, and commitment to data accuracy and integrity.

Project managers should establish clear baseline plans, define work packages, and allocate resources accurately to ensure the validity and reliability of EVM measurements.

By leveraging Earned Value Management, project managers can gain valuable insights into project performance, make proactive decisions, and ultimately improve project outcomes. EVM serves as a powerful tool for driving project success and delivering value to stakeholders.

Cost Management Software and Tools

Cost management software and tools play a vital role in facilitating the effective planning, monitoring, and control of project costs. In this section, we explore the various types of software and tools available to support cost management activities.

Cost estimating software provides project managers with tools and templates to develop accurate and reliable cost estimates for project activities, resources, and deliverables.

These software solutions often include features such as parametric estimating, historical data analysis, and built-in cost models to streamline the estimation process and improve accuracy.

Project Management Information Systems (PMIS) are comprehensive software platforms designed to support project management activities, including cost management.

PMIS typically integrate cost management functionalities with other project management processes, such as scheduling, resource management, and reporting, to provide a holistic view of project performance.

Benefits of Cost Management Software and Tools:

• Increased Efficiency: Cost management software automates repetitive tasks, reduces manual effort, and streamlines the cost estimation, budgeting, and control processes, thereby improving overall efficiency.

• Enhanced Accuracy: By leveraging built-in cost models, historical data analysis, and advanced algorithms, cost management software helps improve the accuracy and reliability of cost estimates, reducing the likelihood of cost overruns.

• Better Decision-Making: Cost management tools provide

project managers with real-time visibility into project costs, performance metrics, and trends, enabling data-driven decision-making and proactive risk management.

• **Improved Collaboration:** Many cost management software solutions offer collaboration features such as document sharing, task assignments, and communication tools, facilitating collaboration among project team members and stakeholders.

Considerations for Selecting Cost Management Software:

Features and Functionality: Assess the features and functionality offered by cost management software to ensure they align with your project's specific requirements and workflows.

Integration Capabilities: Consider the integration capabilities of cost management software with other project management tools and systems used within your organization to ensure seamless data exchange and workflow integration.

User-Friendliness: Evaluate the user interface, ease of use, and learning curve associated with cost management software to ensure adoption and usability among project team members.

Cost and Scalability: Consider the cost, licensing model, and scalability of cost management software to ensure it fits within your organization's budget and can accommodate future growth and expansion.

By leveraging cost management software and tools effectively, project managers can streamline cost management processes, improve accuracy and efficiency, and ultimately enhance project success and stakeholder satisfaction.

Challenges and Best Practices

Now, we examine the common challenges encountered in cost management and explore best practices for addressing them effectively. By understanding these challenges and adopting best practices, project managers can enhance their ability to manage project costs and achieve successful project outcomes.

Common Challenges in Cost Management include:

Uncertain Requirements: Shifting project requirements and scope changes can make accurate cost estimation and budgeting challenging, leading to cost overruns and schedule delays.

Resource Constraints: Limited availability of skilled labour, materials, or financial resources can impact project cost and schedule, requiring careful resource allocation and optimization.

Scope Creep: Uncontrolled scope creep, where project scope expands beyond the initial plan without corresponding adjustments to the budget and schedule, can lead to budget overruns and project delays.

External Factors: External factors such as market volatility, regulatory changes, and economic uncertainties can impact project costs and require adaptive cost management strategies.

Invest time and effort in thorough project planning, including comprehensive cost estimation, budgeting, and risk assessment, to establish a solid foundation for effective cost management.

Implement regular monitoring and control mechanisms to track project costs against the budget, identify variances, and take corrective actions proactively to prevent cost overruns.

Integrate risk management processes into cost management activities to identify, assess, and mitigate risks that may impact project costs, schedule, or quality.

Engage stakeholders throughout the project lifecycle to ensure alignment of cost management objectives with project goals, expectations, and constraints.

Leverage cost management software, tools, and techniques such as Earned Value Management (EVM), parametric estimation, and data analytics to improve accuracy, efficiency, and visibility into project costs.

Implement robust change management processes to address scope changes, variations, and unforeseen events effectively, ensuring that changes are rigorously evaluated, approved, and integrated into the project plan.

By adopting these best practices and addressing common challenges proactively, project managers can enhance their ability to manage project costs effectively, minimize risks, and deliver successful project outcomes that meet stakeholder expectations and objectives.

CHAPTER 2: COST PLANNING

Introduction to Cost Planning

Cost planning serves as the bedrock of project management, providing a roadmap for effective resource allocation and financial stewardship. In this section, we delve into the pivotal role of cost planning, illuminating its significance in the project lifecycle and its alignment with broader organizational objectives.

Cost planning stands as a linchpin in the project management process, acting as a compass that guides decision-making and resource allocation. By meticulously forecasting and budgeting for expenses, organizations can mitigate financial risks, optimize resource utilization, and ensure project feasibility. Moreover, effective cost planning instils confidence among stakeholders, fostering trust and transparency in project execution.

At its core, cost planning is not merely a tactical exercise but a strategic endeavour that harmonizes with project objectives and organizational aspirations. By aligning cost planning with project goals, organizations can steer resources towards endeavours that drive value and advance strategic priorities. Whether it be enhancing product quality, expanding market reach, or achieving operational efficiencies, cost planning serves as a conduit for translating vision into tangible outcomes.

In essence, cost planning is not an isolated function but an integral component of project management that intertwines with every facet of organizational strategy. As we embark on this exploration of cost planning, let us recognize its transformative potential in shaping project outcomes and propelling organizational success.

Cost Planning Process

Cost planning encapsulates a structured and systematic approach to forecasting, budgeting, and managing project expenditures. In this section, we unravel the intricate layers of the cost planning process, delineating the sequential steps essential for effective cost management.

1. Identifying Cost Components and Variables

At the genesis of the cost planning process lies a meticulous examination of all pertinent cost components and variables. This entails a comprehensive analysis of labour, materials, equipment, overheads, contingencies, and any other expenses intrinsic to the project. By scrutinizing these elements with precision, project managers can establish a holistic understanding of the financial landscape and anticipate potential cost drivers.

2. Estimating Costs

With a clear delineation of cost components in hand, the next imperative is to estimate costs with accuracy and foresight. Various techniques, such as analogous estimating, parametric estimating, and bottom-up estimating, serve as invaluable tools in this endeavour. Drawing upon historical data, expert judgment, and industry benchmarks, project managers embark on the intricate task of quantifying costs across all project dimensions.

3. Developing a Cost Baseline and Budget

Central to the cost planning process is the formulation of a robust cost baseline and budget that serves as a beacon for financial governance. The cost baseline delineates the planned expenditure trajectory over time, providing a reference point for monitoring and controlling costs. Concurrently, the budget allocates financial resources to specific activities or work packages, ensuring alignment with project objectives and resource constraints.

4. Incorporating Risk Assessment and Contingency Planning

In the dynamic realm of project management, uncertainty looms as an omnipresent force that necessitates proactive risk management. Thus, the cost planning process encompasses a judicious assessment of potential risks and contingencies that may impact project costs. By identifying, evaluating, and mitigating risks, project managers fortify the cost baseline against unforeseen disruptions, safeguarding project viability and resilience.

In essence, the cost planning process embodies a meticulous orchestration of financial foresight, strategic alignment, and risk mitigation. As project managers navigate through its intricacies, they wield a potent instrument for steering projects towards success while preserving fiscal integrity and organizational sustainability.

Cost Budgeting

Cost budgeting serves as a pivotal phase in the cost planning process, providing a structured framework for allocating financial resources and tracking expenditures throughout the project lifecycle. In this section, we explore the intricacies of cost budgeting and its paramount importance in ensuring project viability and financial accountability.

1. Allocation of Financial Resources

Cost budgeting commences with the allocation of financial resources to various project activities, tasks, or work packages. This entails translating the cost estimates derived from the estimation process into tangible budgetary allocations. Project managers collaborate with stakeholders to delineate funding priorities and allocate resources in alignment with project objectives, scope, and timeline.

2. Development of a Cost Baseline

Central to cost budgeting is the formulation of a cost baseline—a snapshot of planned expenditures over time. The cost baseline serves as a benchmark against which actual costs are measured and monitored throughout the project lifecycle. By establishing a clear trajectory of anticipated costs, project managers gain visibility into the financial health of the project and can proactively identify deviations from the plan.

3. Tracking Budgeted Versus Actual Costs

Once the cost baseline is established, project managers embark on the ongoing task of tracking budgeted versus actual costs. This entails monitoring expenditures in real-time and comparing them against the budgeted amounts. Discrepancies between budgeted and actual costs serve as early warning signals, prompting corrective action and enabling timely interventions to mitigate cost overruns or deviations from the plan.

4. Incorporation of Contingency Planning

Cost budgeting also incorporates provisions for contingency planning—an essential component for managing uncertainty and mitigating risks. Contingency reserves are set aside to address unforeseen events or changes in project scope that may impact costs. By incorporating contingency planning into the budgeting process, project managers ensure financial resilience and flexibility to respond to evolving circumstances without jeopardizing project objectives.

5. Stakeholder Communication and Accountability

Effective cost budgeting necessitates clear and transparent communication with stakeholders regarding budgetary allocations, expenditures, and variances. Project managers are tasked with fostering a culture of financial accountability and ownership among project team members, contractors, and other stakeholders. Regular budget updates and reporting mechanisms enable stakeholders to stay informed and engaged, fostering trust and collaboration throughout the project lifecycle.

In essence, cost budgeting serves as a linchpin in the cost planning process, providing a structured framework for allocating, monitoring, and controlling project expenditures. By adhering to sound budgeting practices and fostering collaboration among stakeholders, project managers can navigate the complexities of cost management with confidence and ensure the successful delivery of projects within budgetary constraints.

Risk Management in Cost Planning

Cost planning operates within a dynamic environment fraught with uncertainties and potential risks. In this section, we delve into the critical role of risk management within the cost planning process, elucidating strategies for identifying, assessing, and mitigating cost-related risks to ensure project success and financial stability.

1. Identification of Cost-Related Risks

Risk management in cost planning begins with a comprehensive identification of potential risks that could impact project costs. These risks may arise from various sources, including market volatility, resource shortages, scope changes, regulatory compliance, and unforeseen events such as natural disasters or geopolitical instability. Project managers collaborate with stakeholders to conduct risk assessments and compile a comprehensive risk register that catalogues potential threats to the project budget.

2. Qualitative and Quantitative Risk Assessment

Following risk identification, project managers conduct qualitative and quantitative assessments to evaluate the likelihood and potential impact of identified risks. Qualitative assessments involve assigning probability and severity ratings to each risk, while quantitative assessments quantify the financial impact of risks in monetary terms. Through these assessments, project managers gain insights into the overall risk exposure of the project and prioritize mitigation efforts accordingly.

3. Development of Risk Response Strategies

Armed with a clear understanding of project risks, project managers formulate risk response strategies to proactively address and mitigate potential threats to the project budget. These strategies may include risk avoidance, risk mitigation, risk transfer, or acceptance, depending on the nature and severity of the risks identified. By developing robust risk response plans, project managers enhance the project's resilience and minimize the likelihood and impact of cost overruns.

4. Contingency Planning and Reserve Allocation

Contingency planning plays a crucial role in cost management by providing a buffer against unforeseen events and risks that may impact project costs. Project managers allocate contingency reserves—additional funds set aside specifically to address identified risks and uncertainties. These reserves serve as a financial safety net, enabling project managers to respond promptly to emerging risks without compromising project objectives or exhausting the primary project budget.

5. Continuous Monitoring and Adaptation

Risk management is an iterative process that requires continuous monitoring and adaptation throughout the project lifecycle. Project managers regularly review and reassess the project's risk profile, updating risk registers and response plans as new risks emerge or existing risks evolve. By maintaining vigilance and adaptability, project managers safeguard the project budget and ensure its alignment with evolving project conditions and stakeholder expectations.

In conclusion, risk management is an integral component of cost planning, enabling project managers to anticipate, assess, and mitigate potential threats to the project budget. By integrating risk management principles into the cost planning process, project managers enhance financial resilience, foster stakeholder confidence, and maximize the likelihood of project success in the face of uncertainty.

Integration with Schedule Planning

Cost planning and schedule planning are intricately intertwined aspects of project management, each exerting a profound influence on the other. In this section, we explore the symbiotic relationship between cost planning and schedule planning, elucidating strategies for seamless integration to optimize project outcomes and ensure alignment with organizational objectives.

1. Alignment of Cost and Schedule Objectives

The integration of cost planning with schedule planning begins with a harmonization of project objectives across both domains. Project managers collaborate with stakeholders to establish clear, measurable goals that reflect not only cost constraints but also schedule constraints. By aligning cost and schedule objectives from the outset, project managers lay the foundation for cohesive planning and execution that drives project success.

2. Development of the Cost-Schedule Baseline

A key milestone in the integration of cost and schedule planning is the development of the cost-schedule baseline —a unified framework that synchronizes cost and schedule projections over the project lifecycle. The cost-schedule baseline serves as a comprehensive roadmap that delineates the planned expenditure trajectory in tandem with the project timeline. By consolidating cost and schedule data into a single integrated baseline, project managers enhance visibility, accountability, and decision-making efficacy.

3. Resource Levelling and Optimization

Effective integration of cost and schedule planning entails optimizing resource allocation to balance cost considerations with schedule constraints. Project managers employ resource levelling techniques to distribute resources evenly over the project timeline, thereby minimizing peaks and valleys in resource utilization. By smoothing resource utilization patterns, project managers optimize cost efficiency, mitigate resource bottlenecks, and enhance schedule adherence without compromising project objectives.

4. Earned Value Management (EVM)

Earned Value Management (EVM) serves as a cornerstone in the integration of cost and schedule planning, providing a robust framework for assessing project performance against planned cost and schedule baselines. By measuring progress in terms of earned value—a quantification of the value of work completed—project managers gain insights into cost and schedule variances, schedule performance, and cost efficiency. EVM enables project managers to identify deviations from the plan early, enabling timely interventions to mitigate risks and optimize project outcomes.

5. Continuous Monitoring and Adjustment

Integration of cost and schedule planning is an ongoing process that requires continuous monitoring, evaluation, and adjustment throughout the project lifecycle. Project managers employ performance metrics, trend analysis, and variance analysis to assess project progress against planned cost and schedule baselines continually. By identifying deviations from the plan in real-time, project managers can implement corrective actions promptly, optimize resource allocation, and maintain alignment with project objectives.

In summary, integration of cost and schedule planning

is essential for optimizing project outcomes, enhancing resource efficiency, and ensuring alignment with organizational objectives. By fostering collaboration between cost and schedule stakeholders and employing robust planning and monitoring mechanisms, project managers can navigate the complexities of project execution with confidence and deliver successful outcomes within cost and schedule constraints.

Cost Planning Tools and Software

Cost planning tools and software play a pivotal role in streamlining the cost planning process, enhancing accuracy, efficiency, and collaboration among project stakeholders. In this section, we explore the diverse array of tools and software applications available to support cost planning activities and optimize project outcomes.

1. Cost Estimation Software

Cost estimation software offers sophisticated algorithms and databases to streamline the process of estimating project costs. These tools leverage historical data, industry benchmarks, and parametric models to generate accurate and reliable cost estimates across various project dimensions. From simple spreadsheet-based solutions to advanced software packages, cost estimation software empowers project managers to make informed decisions and develop robust cost baselines.

2. Project Management Software

Project management software serves as a central hub for coordinating cost planning activities, schedule management, resource allocation, and communication among project team members. These platforms offer features such as budget tracking, resource levelling, Gantt charts, and collaboration tools to facilitate seamless integration of cost and schedule planning. By centralizing project data and workflows, project management software enhances visibility, accountability, and decision-making efficacy throughout the project lifecycle.

3. Earned Value Management (EVM) Tools

Earned Value Management (EVM) tools provide comprehensive frameworks and dashboards for implementing and monitoring EVM principles in cost planning activities. These tools integrate cost, schedule, and performance data to calculate key performance indicators (KPIs) such as Cost Performance Index (CPI), Schedule Performance Index (SPI), and Estimate at Completion (EAC). By visualizing project performance metrics in real-time, EVM tools enable project managers to identify trends, assess risks, and make data-driven decisions to optimize project outcomes.

4. Building Information Modelling (BIM) Software

Building Information Modelling (BIM) software revolutionizes cost planning for construction projects by enabling 3D visualization, collaboration, and data integration across the project lifecycle. BIM platforms facilitate accurate quantity take-offs, clash detection, and cost estimation based on virtual models of building components. By fostering collaboration among architects, engineers, contractors, and cost estimators, BIM software minimizes errors, reduces rework, and enhances cost certainty in construction projects.

5. Cost Management Modules in Enterprise Resource Planning (ERP) Systems

Enterprise Resource Planning (ERP) systems encompass integrated modules for managing various aspects of project planning, execution, and financial management, including cost planning. These modules offer functionalities such as budgeting, forecasting, cost tracking, and variance analysis to support comprehensive cost management across the organization. By leveraging ERP systems, project managers gain access to centralized data, standardized processes, and robust reporting capabilities to optimize cost planning and financial governance.

In summary, cost planning tools and software empower

project managers to streamline cost estimation, budgeting, and monitoring activities, thereby enhancing accuracy, efficiency, and collaboration throughout the project lifecycle. By leveraging the capabilities of these tools, project managers can navigate the complexities of cost planning with confidence and deliver successful outcomes within budgetary constraints.

Challenges and Best Practices

In this section, we explore the inherent challenges encountered in cost planning and present best practices to address these challenges effectively, ensuring the successful execution of projects and the achievement of cost management objectives.

1. Uncertainty and Complexity

Cost planning often grapples with inherent uncertainties and complexities inherent in project environments. Uncertain market conditions, evolving stakeholder requirements, and dynamic regulatory landscapes pose challenges to accurate cost estimation and budgeting. Best Practice: Embrace Flexibility and Iteration - Adopting agile methodologies and iterative planning approaches enables project teams to adapt to changing circumstances, refine cost estimates, and adjust budgets dynamically based on evolving project conditions.

2. Limited Data and Historical Information

In many cases, cost planning encounters challenges due to limited data availability and historical information, particularly in novel or unique project contexts. Insufficient data can hinder accurate cost estimation and increase the risk of budgetary overruns. Best Practice: Employ Expert Judgment and Analogous Estimating - Leveraging the expertise of subject matter experts and conducting analogous estimating based on similar past projects can provide valuable insights and heuristic guidance for cost estimation in the absence of comprehensive data.

3. Scope Changes and Scope Creep

Scope changes and scope creep present significant challenges to cost planning, as they can introduce additional costs and disrupt budgetary projections. Inadequate scope definition, evolving project requirements, and stakeholder demands contribute to scope volatility and pose risks to cost management efforts. Best Practice: Implement Robust Change Management Processes - Establishing robust change management processes enables project teams to systematically assess, prioritize, and address scope changes, ensuring alignment with project objectives and minimizing cost impacts.

4. Stakeholder Expectations and Communication

Effective stakeholder management and communication are essential components of successful cost planning. Misaligned stakeholder expectations, communication breakdowns, and insufficient engagement can lead to misunderstandings, delays, and budgetary disputes. Best Practice: Foster Transparent Communication and Stakeholder Engagement - Maintaining open channels of communication, proactively managing stakeholder expectations, and soliciting stakeholder input throughout the cost planning process foster trust, collaboration, and alignment with project objectives.

5. Resource Constraints and Budget Limitations

Resource constraints and budget limitations pose significant challenges to cost planning, particularly in projects with tight financial constraints or competing priorities. Limited funding, escalating costs, and budgetary pressures require project teams to optimize resource allocation and prioritize investments judiciously. Best Practice: Prioritize Value-Adding Activities and Risk Management - Prioritizing value-adding activities that align with project objectives and conducting rigorous risk management to identify, assess, and mitigate cost risks enable project teams to optimize resource allocation and preserve budgetary integrity.

In summary, effective cost planning requires an understanding of the challenges inherent in project environments and the adoption of best practices to address these challenges proactively. By embracing flexibility, leveraging expertise, implementing robust change management processes, fostering transparent communication, and optimizing resource allocation, project teams can navigate cost planning challenges successfully and achieve project success within budgetary constraints.

In this chapter, we have delved into the intricacies of cost planning, exploring its fundamental principles, methodologies, and practical applications in project management. From cost estimation and budgeting to risk management and stakeholder communication, cost planning serves as a cornerstone of project success, ensuring financial viability, accountability, and alignment with organizational objectives.

Throughout our exploration, we have encountered various challenges inherent in cost planning, including uncertainty, limited data availability, scope changes, stakeholder expectations, and resource constraints. However, we have also identified best practices and strategies to address these challenges effectively, fostering resilience, adaptability, and innovation in cost management efforts.

By embracing flexibility, leveraging expertise, implementing robust change management processes, fostering transparent communication, and optimizing resource allocation, project teams can navigate cost planning challenges successfully and achieve project success within budgetary constraints. Moreover, by integrating cost planning with schedule planning, risk management, and stakeholder engagement, project managers can orchestrate cohesive planning and execution efforts that drive project success and maximize value for stakeholders.

As we conclude our exploration of cost planning, it is essential to recognize that effective cost management is not merely a technical endeavour but a strategic imperative that underpins organizational success and sustainability. By instilling a culture of financial discipline, accountability, and continuous improvement, organizations can enhance their cost planning capabilities and position themselves for long-term growth and resilience in an ever-evolving business landscape.

In closing, cost planning represents a journey of discovery, collaboration, and innovation—a journey guided by principles of foresight, adaptability, and stewardship. By embracing these principles and applying the insights gleaned from our exploration, project managers can navigate the complexities of cost planning with confidence and deliver superior outcomes that propel their organizations towards excellence and prosperity.

CHAPTER 3: COST CONTROL

Introduction to Cost Control

Cost control stands as a linchpin in the realm of project management, anchoring the fiscal health and success of endeavours across industries. In this introductory section, we unravel the significance of cost control, elucidating its pivotal role in steering projects towards financial stability, adherence to budgetary constraints, and alignment with overarching business objectives.

Cost control emerges as a fundamental aspect of project management, wielding influence over the viability and sustainability of initiatives from inception to completion. By exerting meticulous oversight and governance over project expenditures, cost control endeavours to mitigate financial risks, optimize resource allocation, and safeguard the attainment of project objectives within predefined budgetary thresholds.

Integral to the fabric of cost control is its seamless alignment with project objectives and overarching business goals. As projects unfold amidst dynamic landscapes rife with uncertainties and complexities, cost control serves as a compass, guiding decision-making processes and resource allocations in harmony with strategic imperatives and stakeholder expectations. Whether driving innovation, enhancing operational efficiency, or expanding market reach, cost control remains steadfast in its pursuit of value creation and organizational excellence.

In essence, the introductory exploration of cost control sets the stage for a deeper dive into its intricacies and applications in subsequent sections. By illuminating its overarching significance and strategic relevance, we lay the groundwork for a comprehensive understanding of cost control's transformative potential in navigating the complexities of project management with precision and foresight.

Cost Control Process

Cost control encapsulates a systematic approach to managing project expenditures, ensuring alignment with budgetary constraints and organizational objectives. In this section, we elucidate the multifaceted cost control process, comprising a series of interrelated steps aimed at optimizing financial performance and safeguarding project viability.

1. Identification of Cost Control Objectives and Performance Metrics:

The cost control process commences with a clear delineation of objectives and performance metrics tailored to the project's unique characteristics and stakeholder expectations.

Objectives may encompass targets for cost reduction, variance minimization, resource optimization, or adherence to budgetary constraints, while performance metrics span key performance indicators (KPIs) such as Cost Performance Index (CPI), Schedule Performance Index (SPI), and Estimate at Completion (EAC).

2. Development of a Cost Control Plan:

A robust cost control plan serves as a blueprint for orchestrating cost management efforts throughout the project lifecycle.

The plan outlines strategies, methodologies, roles, and responsibilities for monitoring, tracking, and adjusting project expenditures in alignment with predefined budgetary thresholds and project objectives.

3. Implementation of Cost Control Measures:

With the cost control plan in place, project teams embark on the implementation phase, executing a suite of measures to enforce fiscal discipline and optimize financial performance.

Cost control measures encompass a spectrum of activities, including budget tracking, variance analysis, change management, resource optimization, and risk mitigation, aimed at proactively managing project costs and mitigating deviations from the plan.

The cost control process represents a dynamic and iterative endeavour, characterized by continuous monitoring, evaluation, and adaptation to evolving project conditions and stakeholder expectations. By adhering to a structured approach and leveraging appropriate tools and methodologies, project teams can navigate the complexities of cost control with precision and foresight, driving projects towards successful outcomes within budgetary constraints.

Cost Tracking and Monitoring

Cost tracking and monitoring are pivotal components of effective cost control, providing project teams with the necessary insights to gauge financial performance and address deviations from the budget.

Establishing Baseline Costs and Performance Indicators:

At the outset, project teams establish baseline costs, comprising initial budget allocations and expenditure forecasts outlined in the project plan. These baseline costs serve as reference points against which actual expenditures are measured, facilitating the assessment of performance and identification of deviations from the plan.

Regular Monitoring of Actual Costs Versus Budgeted Costs:

Throughout the project lifecycle, project teams regularly

monitor actual costs incurred and compare them against budgeted costs to assess variances. This real-time tracking enables teams to identify discrepancies promptly and take corrective actions to ensure alignment with budgetary constraints.

Utilization of Performance Measurement Techniques:

Performance measurement techniques like Earned Value Management (EVM), variance analysis, and trend analysis are leveraged to evaluate cost performance and forecast future expenditures. EVM, in particular, integrates cost, schedule, and scope data to calculate key performance indicators such as Cost Performance Index (CPI), Schedule Performance Index (SPI), and Estimate at Completion (EAC), providing valuable insights into cost efficiency and schedule adherence.

Cost tracking and monitoring are iterative processes, demanding continuous vigilance and adaptation to changing project conditions. By employing rigorous monitoring mechanisms and leveraging performance measurement techniques, project teams can maintain fiscal discipline, optimize resource utilization, and steer projects towards successful outcomes within budgetary constraints.

Change Management and Scope Control

Change management and scope control are integral facets of cost control, aimed at managing scope changes and minimizing their impact on project costs. In this section, we explore the methodologies and strategies employed to effectively manage changes to project scope while preserving budgetary integrity.

1. Identification and Evaluation of Scope Changes:

Identifying and evaluating scope changes is the first step in change management and scope control. Project teams must establish robust mechanisms for capturing and assessing proposed changes to project scope, including evaluating their impact on project objectives, deliverables, and costs.

2. Implementation of Robust Change Management Processes:

Robust change management processes are essential for effectively managing scope changes and minimizing their impact on project costs. These processes include formal procedures for requesting, evaluating, approving, and implementing scope changes, as well as mechanisms for communicating changes to relevant stakeholders.

3. Integration of Scope Control Measures with Cost Tracking:

Integrating scope control measures with cost tracking mechanisms enables project teams to monitor the financial impact of scope changes in real-time. By aligning cost tracking with scope control, project managers can assess the cost implications of proposed changes and make informed decisions regarding their approval or rejection.

Change management and scope control are ongoing processes that require continuous monitoring and adaptation throughout the project lifecycle. By implementing robust change management processes, integrating scope control measures with cost tracking mechanisms, and fostering transparent communication with stakeholders, project teams can effectively manage scope changes and preserve budgetary integrity, ensuring successful project outcomes within predefined budgetary constraints.

Resource Optimization and Efficiency

Resource optimization and efficiency are central to effective cost control, enabling project teams to maximize the value of resources while minimizing wastage and inefficiencies. In this section, we explore strategies and best practices for optimizing resource allocation and enhancing efficiency to achieve cost control objectives.

1. Optimization of Resource Allocation:

Optimal resource allocation involves identifying the most effective and efficient use of resources to support project objectives while minimizing costs. Project teams must carefully evaluate resource requirements, availability, and utilization to ensure that resources are allocated judiciously and aligned with project priorities.

2. Identification and Elimination of Resource Wastage:

Identifying and eliminating resource wastage is essential for cost control, as inefficient resource usage can lead to unnecessary costs and budget overruns. Project teams should conduct regular assessments to identify areas of resource wastage and implement measures to eliminate inefficiencies and streamline processes.

3. Implementation of Lean Principles:

Lean principles, derived from lean manufacturing methodologies, emphasize the elimination of waste and continuous improvement to enhance efficiency and productivity. Project teams can apply lean principles to optimize processes, reduce cycle times, and minimize costs by eliminating non-value-added activities and maximizing resource utilization.

Resource optimization and efficiency require a proactive and systematic approach, involving continuous monitoring, evaluation, and improvement of resource allocation and utilization practices. By optimizing resource allocation, identifying, and eliminating resource wastage, and embracing lean principles, project teams can enhance efficiency, minimize costs, and achieve cost control objectives within budgetary constraints.

Risk Management in Cost Control

Risk management plays a crucial role in cost control, enabling project teams to identify, assess, and mitigate potential threats to project budgets and financial objectives. In this section, we explore the integration of risk management principles and practices into cost control efforts to safeguard project finances and enhance overall project success.

1. Identification and Assessment of Cost-Related Risks:

The first step in risk management in cost control involves identifying and assessing cost-related risks that have the potential to impact project budgets and financial performance. Project teams must conduct comprehensive risk assessments to identify threats such as cost overruns, budget variances, and resource constraints.

2. Development of Risk Response Strategies:

Once risks have been identified and assessed, project teams develop risk response strategies to mitigate their impact on project finances. These strategies may include contingency planning, risk avoidance, risk transfer, and risk mitigation measures aimed at reducing the likelihood and severity of potential cost-related risks.

3. Integration of Risk Management with Cost Tracking and Monitoring:

Integrating risk management with cost tracking and monitoring enables project teams to proactively identify and address emerging risks that may impact project finances. By aligning risk management activities with cost control efforts, project managers can ensure that potential cost-related risks are identified and addressed in a timely manner.

Risk management in cost control requires a proactive and systematic approach, involving ongoing monitoring, evaluation, and adjustment of risk response strategies based on evolving project conditions. By integrating risk management principles and practices into cost control efforts, project teams can enhance their ability to identify, assess, and mitigate potential threats to project budgets and financial objectives, ultimately ensuring the successful delivery of projects within budgetary constraints.

Communication and Stakeholder Engagement

Effective communication and stakeholder engagement are essential components of cost control, facilitating transparency, collaboration, and alignment with project objectives. In this section, we delve into the importance of communication and stakeholder engagement in cost control efforts and explore strategies for fostering effective communication and engagement with project stakeholders.

Transparent communication of cost performance is critical for building trust and confidence among project stakeholders. Project teams must provide timely and accurate updates on cost performance, including actual expenditures, budget variances, and forecasts, to ensure stakeholders are informed of project finances.

Active engagement of stakeholders in cost control initiatives is essential for garnering support and buy-in for cost-saving measures and budgetary decisions. Project teams should involve stakeholders in discussions regarding cost control strategies, solicit their input and feedback, and collaborate on identifying opportunities for cost optimization.

Establishing feedback mechanisms enables project teams to solicit input from stakeholders, address their concerns, and incorporate their feedback into cost control efforts. Feedback mechanisms may include regular stakeholder meetings, surveys, and open forums for stakeholders to express their views and provide input on project finances.

Effective communication and stakeholder engagement require a proactive and inclusive approach, involving regular communication, collaboration, and feedback exchange with project stakeholders. By fostering transparency, involving stakeholders in cost control initiatives, and establishing feedback mechanisms, project teams can enhance stakeholder trust and confidence, promote alignment with project objectives, and ultimately ensure the successful management of project finances within budgetary constraints.

Continuous Improvement and Adaptation

Continuous improvement and adaptation are essential tenets of effective cost control, enabling project teams to refine processes, address emerging challenges, and optimize financial performance throughout the project lifecycle. In this section, we explore the principles of continuous improvement and adaptation in the context of cost control and discuss strategies for fostering a culture of innovation and agility.

1. Evaluation of Cost Control Effectiveness:

Regular evaluation of cost control effectiveness is paramount for identifying areas of improvement and refining cost management practices. Project teams should conduct periodic assessments of cost control processes, performance metrics, and outcomes to gauge effectiveness and identify opportunities for enhancement.

2. Lessons Learned from Past Projects:

Drawing lessons from past projects is instrumental in informing future cost control efforts. Project teams should analyse past project experiences, successes, and challenges to extract valuable insights and best practices that can be applied to current and future endeavours.

3. Implementation of Corrective Actions and Process Improvements:

Based on the findings of evaluations and lessons learned, project teams should implement corrective actions and process improvements to enhance cost control effectiveness. This may involve refining cost estimation methodologies, optimizing resource allocation practices, and streamlining cost tracking and monitoring processes.

4. Adoption of Agile Methodologies and Adaptive Strategies:

Embracing agile methodologies and adaptive strategies enables project teams to respond effectively to changing project conditions and stakeholder requirements. By adopting iterative planning, frequent reassessment, and flexible decision-making, project teams can adapt cost control efforts in real-time to address evolving challenges and opportunities.

Continuous improvement and adaptation in cost control require a proactive and iterative approach, involving ongoing assessment, learning, and adjustment of cost management practices. By fostering a culture of innovation, embracing lessons learned from past projects, implementing corrective actions, and adopting agile methodologies, project teams can enhance their ability to optimize financial performance, mitigate risks, and ensure the successful delivery of projects within budgetary constraints.

Challenges and Best Practices

In this section, we examine the common challenges encountered in cost control efforts and present best practices to overcome these obstacles and optimize financial performance.

1. Uncertainty and Complexity:

Overview: The inherent uncertainty and complexity of projects pose significant challenges to effective cost control.

Best Practices: Implement robust risk management processes, conduct thorough risk assessments, and develop contingency plans to mitigate potential cost-related risks.

2. Scope Changes and Creep:

Overview: Scope changes and scope creep can disrupt project budgets and timelines, leading to cost overruns.

Best Practices: Establish rigorous change management processes, communicate scope changes transparently, and conduct impact assessments to evaluate the financial implications of proposed changes.

3. Resource Constraints:

Overview: Limited resources and budgetary constraints can hinder cost control efforts and impede project success.

Best Practices: Optimize resource allocation, prioritize critical activities, and explore alternative sourcing options to maximize resource efficiency and minimize costs.

4. Stakeholder Resistance:

Overview: Stakeholder resistance to cost control measures can undermine project finances and impede progress.

Best Practices: Foster stakeholder engagement, communicate the rationale behind cost control initiatives, and solicit stakeholder input to gain buy-in and support for cost-saving measures.

5. Proactive Monitoring and Reporting:

Overview: Proactive monitoring and reporting of project costs are essential for identifying cost variances and taking timely corrective actions.

Best Practices: Utilize robust cost tracking mechanisms, implement real-time reporting tools, and establish regular review processes to track project finances and ensure alignment with budgetary constraints.

6. Continuous Improvement:

Overview: Continuous improvement fosters innovation and enhances cost control effectiveness over time.

Best Practices: Encourage a culture of learning and innovation, conduct regular performance reviews, and solicit feedback from project teams to identify opportunities for process refinement and optimization.

By addressing common challenges with best practices and proactive approaches, project teams can overcome obstacles to cost control and optimize financial performance, ultimately ensuring the successful delivery of projects within budgetary constraints.

In this concluding section, we reflect on the key concepts and insights gleaned from our exploration of cost control principles and practices. We underscore the importance of cost control in project management and highlight the critical role it plays in achieving project success within budgetary constraints.

Throughout this chapter, we have delved into various facets of cost control, from the establishment of baseline costs and performance indicators to the implementation of risk management strategies and continuous improvement initiatives. We have examined the challenges encountered in cost control efforts and presented best practices to overcome these obstacles and optimize financial performance.

Mastering cost control is essential for ensuring the successful delivery of projects within budgetary constraints. By adopting a proactive and systematic approach to cost management, project teams can mitigate financial risks, optimize resource allocation, and enhance project outcomes.

As we conclude our exploration of cost control, we urge project teams to implement the insights and best practices discussed in this chapter. By fostering a culture of cost consciousness, embracing innovation, and continuously striving for improvement, project teams can enhance their ability to manage project finances effectively and achieve successful outcomes.

In closing, cost control is not merely a function of project management but a strategic imperative for organizations seeking to maximize value and achieve sustainable growth. By prioritizing cost control efforts and integrating them into project management processes, organizations can navigate the complexities of project delivery with confidence and achieve their strategic objectives within budgetary constraints.

CHAPTER 4: RISK MANAGEMENT AND COST

Introduction to Risk Management and Cost

Risk management and cost are inseparable elements within the realm of project management. In this section, we embark on an exploration of how risk management practices intertwine with cost considerations to shape the financial landscape of projects.

Effective risk management is essential for mitigating potential threats to project budgets and financial objectives. By identifying, assessing, and mitigating risks, project teams can safeguard against cost overruns, delays, and other financial setbacks that may jeopardize project success.

Risk management practices exert a profound influence on project finances throughout the project lifecycle. From the identification of cost-related risks to the implementation of mitigation strategies, each phase of the risk management process has implications for project costs. By proactively managing risks, project teams can minimize the financial impact of unforeseen events and uncertainties, thereby enhancing the likelihood of project success within budgetary constraints.

In essence, the introduction to risk management and cost sets the stage for a comprehensive exploration of how risk management practices shape project finances and influence cost control efforts. By understanding the interplay between risk management and cost, project teams can develop proactive strategies to mitigate risks, optimize financial performance, and achieve project success.

Identifying Cost-Related Risks

Cost-related risks lurk in various facets of project management, potentially disrupting financial plans and derailing project success. In this section, we delve into methodologies for identifying these risks and understanding their implications on project finances.

Effective identification of cost-related risks necessitates a systematic approach. Project teams employ various techniques such as brainstorming sessions, expert interviews, historical data analysis, and risk checklists to unearth potential threats to project budgets. Risks are categorized based on their impact on project costs, such as labour cost overruns, material price fluctuations, scope changes, and unforeseen expenses.

Examples of Common Cost-Related Risks in Project Management:

- Labor Cost Overruns: Unforeseen increases in labour costs due to overtime, wage inflation, or skill shortages.
- Material Price Fluctuations: Volatility in the prices of raw materials or commodities, impacting procurement budgets.
- Scope Changes: Changes in project scope leading to additional work and associated costs.
- Currency Exchange Rate Risks: Fluctuations in exchange rates affecting project costs for multinational projects.
- Regulatory Compliance Costs: Unexpected expenses arising from changes in regulations or compliance requirements.

By systematically identifying and categorizing cost-related risks, project teams can proactively address potential threats to project finances and develop mitigation strategies to safeguard against cost overruns and budgetary deviations.

Assessing and Prioritizing Cost Risks

Assessing and prioritizing cost risks are pivotal steps in the risk management process, enabling project teams to focus their efforts on addressing the most significant threats to project finances. In this section, we explore techniques for evaluating the likelihood and impact of cost risks and prioritizing them based on their potential consequences.

Probability and Impact Matrix: Project teams assess the likelihood and impact of cost risks and plot them on a matrix to prioritize their attention. Risks with high likelihood and significant impact are given top priority for mitigation.

Quantitative Analysis: Utilizing historical data, statistical models, and simulation techniques to quantitatively assess the likelihood and impact of cost risks. This approach provides a more precise understanding of the potential financial implications of each risk.

Expert Judgment: Drawing on the expertise of project stakeholders, subject matter experts, and industry professionals to qualitatively assess cost risks and their potential impact on project finances.

Risk Scoring: Assigning scores to cost risks based on their likelihood and impact and prioritizing those with the highest scores for immediate attention.

Risk Appetite and Tolerance: Considering the organization's risk appetite and tolerance levels when prioritizing cost risks. Risks that exceed acceptable thresholds are prioritized for mitigation.

Cost-Benefit Analysis: Evaluating the potential cost of mitigating each risk against the potential financial impact of its occurrence to determine the most cost-effective risk mitigation strategies.

By systematically assessing and prioritizing cost risks, project teams can allocate resources effectively and focus their mitigation efforts on addressing the most critical threats to project finances. This proactive approach enhances the likelihood of project success by minimizing the impact of cost-related uncertainties and deviations from budgetary constraints.

Mitigation Strategies for Cost Risks

Mitigation strategies are pivotal in the realm of risk management, especially when it comes to preserving project budgets. Here, we delve into the nuanced approaches to mitigating cost risks, safeguarding financial objectives, and ensuring project success.

Risk Avoidance: This strategy entails steering clear of activities or scenarios that harbour significant cost risks. For instance, opting for standardized components over custom-made parts can mitigate the risk of supply chain disruptions and cost escalations associated with specialized materials.

Risk Transfer: In this approach, the financial burden of cost risks is shifted to external parties through mechanisms like insurance. For example, procuring insurance policies can cover potential cost overruns stemming from adverse weather conditions or labour disputes, providing a safety net for project finances.

Risk Reduction: Mitigation efforts aim to diminish the likelihood or impact of cost risks. For instance, investing in workforce training programs can enhance productivity, reducing the risk of labour cost overruns by ensuring efficient utilization of resources.

Risk Acceptance: Acknowledging the existence of cost risks while opting not to implement specific mitigation measures. Instead, contingency reserves are allocated in the project budget to absorb unexpected cost overruns within predefined limits, allowing for flexibility in budget management.

Integrating Risk Management with Cost Control

Integrating risk management practices with cost control efforts is imperative for maintaining project financial stability and mitigating unforeseen financial risks. Here, we explore the synergies between risk management and cost control, elucidating strategies for seamless integration and proactive financial management.

Strategies for Integration:

1. Holistic Risk Identification: Integrating risk management into cost control begins with a comprehensive risk identification process. Project teams should adopt a holistic approach, considering all potential risks that could impact project finances, including labour cost fluctuations, supply chain disruptions, and scope changes.

2. Risk-Informed Budgeting: Risk-informed budgeting involves incorporating potential cost risks into the project budget from the outset. By allocating contingency reserves and allowances for known risks, project budgets become more resilient to unexpected financial challenges, ensuring greater financial predictability throughout the project lifecycle.

3. Proactive Risk Monitoring: Integrating risk management with cost control requires proactive monitoring of identified risks and their potential impact on project finances. Regular risk assessments and monitoring mechanisms enable project teams to identify emerging risks, assess their implications on project costs, and take timely corrective actions to mitigate financial risks.

4. Contingency Planning: Effective integration of risk management and cost control involves developing robust contingency plans to address identified risks. Contingency plans outline predefined responses to potential risk events, including mitigation strategies, alternative courses of action, and resource allocation adjustments to minimize financial disruptions and ensure project success.

Benefits of Integration:

- Enhanced Financial Predictability: By integrating risk management with cost control, project teams gain greater visibility into potential financial risks, allowing for more accurate budget forecasting and financial planning.

- Improved Decision-Making: Integrated risk management empowers project teams to make informed decisions regarding resource allocation, project prioritization, and risk mitigation strategies based on their potential impact on project finances.

- Minimized Financial Losses: Proactive risk management practices integrated with cost control efforts help minimize financial losses associated with unexpected events or disruptions, ensuring project budgets are safeguarded against unforeseen financial risks.

Integrating risk management with cost control is essential for ensuring project financial stability and resilience in the face of uncertainty. By adopting proactive risk management practices and integrating them into cost control efforts, project teams can enhance financial predictability, minimize financial risks, and ensure the successful delivery of projects within budgetary constraints.

Continuous Monitoring and Adaptation

Continuous monitoring and adaptation are integral components of effective risk management and cost control, allowing project teams to respond promptly to evolving project conditions and financial risks. This section delves into the importance of ongoing vigilance and adaptability in maintaining project financial stability.

Continuous monitoring of project finances and associated risks is essential for staying abreast of changing circumstances and proactively addressing emerging challenges. Regular reviews of cost performance metrics, risk registers, and project progress enable project teams to identify deviations from the plan and take corrective actions in a timely manner.

Real-time risk assessment involves the ongoing evaluation of identified risks and their potential impact on project finances. By leveraging data analytics, key performance indicators, and risk management tools, project teams can conduct dynamic risk assessments to anticipate and mitigate financial risks as they arise, ensuring proactive risk management and cost control.

Adaptive Strategies for Risk Mitigation:

Adaptive strategies entail adjusting risk management and cost control measures in response to changing project conditions and emerging risks. Project teams should remain flexible and agile, ready to adapt their mitigation strategies based on evolving circumstances, new information, and lessons learned from past experiences.

Iterative Improvement:

Continuous monitoring and adaptation facilitate iterative improvement in risk management and cost control practices. By analysing past performance, identifying areas for enhancement, and implementing corrective actions, project teams can refine their approaches over time, enhancing their ability to mitigate financial risks and optimize project outcomes.

Continuous monitoring and adaptation are essential for effective risk management and cost control in project management. By remaining vigilant, proactive, and adaptive, project teams can anticipate and mitigate financial risks, ensuring project financial stability and success in dynamic and uncertain environments.

Challenges and Best Practices

In the realm of risk management and cost control, project teams encounter a myriad of challenges, but with them come opportunities for implementing best practices. Let's explore these challenges and the corresponding strategies for overcoming them seamlessly.

Dynamic Market Conditions: The ever-changing landscape of market conditions, marked by fluctuating commodity prices and regulatory shifts, poses a constant challenge in accurately forecasting project costs and managing financial risks.

Scope Creep: As project requirements evolve over time, managing scope changes becomes crucial to avoid cost overruns and delays, necessitating agile management strategies to stay aligned with project objectives.

Resource Limitations: With constrained resources, including budgetary constraints and workforce shortages, implementing proactive risk management measures can prove challenging, demanding innovative approaches to optimize resource utilization.

Integration Hurdles: Integrating risk management practices with cost control efforts often entails navigating complexity across stakeholders and project teams, requiring cohesive alignment of objectives and priorities to ensure effective coordination.

Proactive Risk Identification: Adopting a forward-thinking approach to risk identification empowers teams to anticipate potential threats by leveraging historical data, expert insights, and advanced risk analysis techniques.

Continuous Monitoring and Adaptation: Establishing robust monitoring mechanisms enables real-time tracking of project costs and risks, facilitating swift responses to emerging challenges and opportunities as they arise.

Stakeholder Collaboration: Fostering a culture of open communication and collaboration among stakeholders ensures alignment of goals, fostering effective risk management and cost control strategies throughout the project lifecycle.

Risk-Informed Decision Making: Integrating risk considerations into decision-making processes allows teams to evaluate the financial implications of various options, enabling informed choices that optimize project outcomes within budget constraints.

Iterative Learning: Embracing a mindset of continuous improvement empowers teams to learn from past experiences, refine practices based on industry standards, and drive innovation in risk management and cost control efforts.

While challenges may abound, they serve as catalysts for innovation and growth when met with effective best practices. By navigating dynamic market conditions, managing scope changes, optimizing resources, and fostering stakeholder collaboration, project teams can overcome obstacles and achieve financial stability while optimizing project outcomes.

In the intricate interplay between risk management and cost control, this journey has unveiled numerous insights and strategies vital for project success. As we draw this exploration to a close, let's reflect on the key takeaways and implications for future endeavours.

Throughout this exploration, we've unearthed the critical role of proactive risk management in safeguarding project finances and ensuring successful project outcomes. From identifying potential risks to implementing mitigation strategies and adapting to changing project conditions, each step in the risk management process is essential for maintaining financial stability and achieving project goals.

Looking ahead, the lessons learned from this journey hold significant implications for future projects. Embracing a proactive approach to risk management, integrating risk considerations into decision-making processes, and fostering collaboration among stakeholders will be essential for navigating uncertainties and optimizing project outcomes.

As we embark on future endeavours, let us heed the lessons learned from this exploration and embrace a culture of continuous improvement in risk management and cost control practices. By fostering innovation, collaboration, and adaptability, we can navigate challenges effectively, optimize project finances, and achieve success within budgetary constraints.

In the dynamic landscape of project management, risk management and cost control serve as pillars of financial stability and project success. By embracing proactive risk management practices, leveraging best practices, and fostering a culture of continuous improvement, project teams can navigate uncertainties adeptly and ensure the successful delivery of projects within budgetary constraints.

CHAPTER 5: VALUE ENGINEERING

Introduction to Value Engineering

Value Engineering (VE) is a systematic approach aimed at maximizing the value of a product, process, or service while minimizing costs. In this section, we delve into the foundational principles of Value Engineering and its significance in the realm of project cost management.

Value Engineering is not merely about reducing costs; rather, it focuses on optimizing the value derived from resources invested in a project. It involves a structured methodology that systematically analyses functions to identify opportunities for improving value, enhancing performance, and reducing unnecessary expenditures.

Importance of Value Engineering:

Value Engineering plays a pivotal role in project cost management by:

• Identifying inefficiencies and redundancies in project processes.

• Generating innovative solutions to optimize project outcomes.

• Enhancing the overall value proposition of a project by aligning resources with project objectives.

• Providing a systematic framework for achieving cost savings without compromising quality or performance.

By embracing Value Engineering principles, project teams can unlock hidden value, streamline project processes, and achieve significant cost savings, thereby enhancing project efficiency and competitiveness. Throughout this chapter, we will explore the principles, processes, applications, and benefits of Value Engineering, shedding light on its role as a cornerstone of effective project cost management.

Principles of Value Engineering

Value Engineering operates on a set of fundamental principles that guide its systematic approach to optimizing value while minimizing costs. In this section, we explore the core principles that underpin the practice of Value Engineering.

1. Understanding the Concept of Value:

At the heart of Value Engineering lies the concept of value, which encompasses the functionality, quality, and performance of a product, process, or service relative to its cost. Value is not solely determined by price but rather by the benefits derived from the investment. Understanding and defining value is essential for effectively identifying opportunities for improvement and cost optimization.

2. Identifying Value-Added and Non-Value-Added Activities:

Value Engineering entails distinguishing between activities that add value to a project and those that do not. Value-added activities directly contribute to meeting project objectives and customer requirements, while non-value-added activities represent waste or inefficiency. By identifying and eliminating non-value-added activities, Value Engineering aims to streamline processes and optimize resource utilization.

3. Cost-Benefit Analysis in Value Engineering:

A cornerstone of Value Engineering is the use of cost-benefit analysis to evaluate potential changes and improvements. Cost-benefit analysis involves quantifying the costs associated with implementing a change or recommendation and comparing them to the anticipated benefits. This analysis helps prioritize initiatives based on their potential return on investment and ensures that proposed changes align with project objectives and budget constraints.

These principles form the foundation of Value Engineering, guiding project teams in their quest to maximize value and minimize costs. By adhering to these principles, project teams can systematically identify opportunities for improvement, optimize resource allocation, and achieve significant cost savings while enhancing project outcomes. Throughout the remainder of this chapter, we will delve deeper into the Value Engineering process, exploring techniques for generating cost-saving ideas and implementing recommendations effectively.

Value Engineering Process

The Value Engineering process is a structured methodology designed to systematically identify opportunities for improving value and reducing costs in projects. In this section, we outline the steps involved in the Value Engineering process.

1. Information Gathering:

The first step in the Value Engineering process is to gather relevant information about the project, including its objectives, requirements, constraints, and current processes. This involves reviewing project documentation, conducting interviews with stakeholders, and analysing existing data to gain a comprehensive understanding of the project's scope and context.

2. Functional Analysis:

Functional analysis involves breaking down the project into its core functions or components and examining the relationships between them. This step aims to identify the essential functions that must be preserved to meet project objectives and those that can be modified or eliminated to improve value and reduce costs.

3. Creative Idea Generation:

Once the project functions have been identified, the next step is to brainstorm creative ideas for improving value and reducing costs. This can involve techniques such as brainstorming sessions, mind mapping, and idea generation workshops, where project team members collaborate to generate innovative solutions to project challenges.

4. Evaluation and Selection:

After generating a list of potential ideas, the next step is to evaluate and prioritize them based on their feasibility, impact on project objectives, and potential cost savings. This may involve conducting cost-benefit analyses, feasibility studies, and risk assessments to assess the potential risks and benefits of each idea.

5. Implementation Planning:

Once the most promising ideas have been selected, the final step is to develop a plan for implementing them. This may involve defining specific action steps, assigning responsibilities, establishing timelines, and allocating resources to ensure successful implementation.

6. Monitoring and Continuous Improvement:

The Value Engineering process does not end with the implementation of ideas. It is essential to monitor the results of the implemented changes continuously and assess their impact on project performance and costs. This feedback loop allows project teams to identify further opportunities for improvement and refine their approaches over time.

The Value Engineering process provides a systematic framework for identifying opportunities for improving value and reducing costs in projects. By following these steps, project teams can systematically analyse project functions, generate innovative solutions, and implement cost-saving ideas effectively, ultimately enhancing project outcomes and maximizing value for stakeholders.

Applications of Value Engineering

Value Engineering transcends industry boundaries, finding relevance in a multitude of sectors and project types. Let's explore how this systematic approach is applied across various domains, each with its unique challenges and opportunities for cost optimization and value enhancement.

Value Engineering in Construction Projects:

In the construction realm, Value Engineering serves as a cornerstone for optimizing project designs, materials, and methodologies. By scrutinizing every aspect of construction projects, from architectural plans to material selections and construction techniques, Value Engineering identifies opportunities for cost savings, performance improvement, and quality enhancement. It ensures that projects achieve optimal outcomes within budgetary constraints while maintaining structural integrity and safety standards.

Value Engineering in Manufacturing Processes:

Within manufacturing industries, Value Engineering drives efficiency, reliability, and cost-effectiveness in production processes. By dissecting manufacturing workflows, analysing production methods, and evaluating resource utilization, Value Engineering uncovers inefficiencies and waste, leading to streamlined operations, enhanced productivity, and improved profitability. It fosters innovation and continuous improvement, empowering manufacturers to stay competitive in dynamic markets.

Value Engineering in Service Industries:

Across service sectors such as healthcare, transportation, and hospitality, Value Engineering revolutionizes service delivery and operational efficiency. It enables service providers to reevaluate processes, optimize resource allocation, and enhance customer experiences while reducing operational costs. Whether it's streamlining patient care pathways, optimizing logistics routes, or improving guest services, Value Engineering drives value creation and operational excellence in service industries.

Value Engineering in Product Development:

In product development, Value Engineering guides the optimization of designs, features, and functionalities to meet customer needs while minimizing manufacturing costs. By conducting rigorous analysis of product specifications, material choices, and production methods, Value Engineering identifies opportunities for design simplification, material substitution, and process optimization. This results in products that offer superior value, performance, and affordability, meeting market demands while maximizing profitability.

Value Engineering in Public Sector Projects:

Government and public sector organizations harness the power of Value Engineering to maximize taxpayer value in public projects and services. From infrastructure development to public services delivery, Value Engineering identifies opportunities for cost savings, efficiency gains, and performance enhancements. It ensures that public investments yield optimal returns, delivering high-quality projects and services that meet the needs of communities while respecting budgetary constraints.

The applications of Value Engineering are as diverse as the industries and sectors it serves, offering a universal framework for optimizing value and minimizing costs in projects of all scales and complexities. By embracing Value Engineering principles and methodologies, organizations across industries can drive innovation, efficiency, and value creation, ensuring sustainable success in an ever-evolving business landscape.

Challenges and Best Practices

Value Engineering, while a powerful tool for optimizing projects, is not without its challenges. In this section, we delve into the common obstacles faced during Value Engineering initiatives and explore best practices for overcoming them effectively.

Resistance to Change: One of the primary challenges in Value Engineering initiatives is resistance to change from stakeholders accustomed to existing processes and procedures. Overcoming this resistance requires effective communication, stakeholder engagement, and demonstrating the benefits of proposed changes.

Limited Resources: Resource constraints, including time, budget, and expertise, can hinder the effectiveness of Value Engineering efforts. Lack of adequate resources may result in incomplete analyses or suboptimal solutions. Addressing resource constraints requires careful planning, prioritization, and leveraging available expertise effectively.

Complexity of Projects: Complex projects with multiple stakeholders, diverse requirements, and intricate processes present unique challenges for Value Engineering initiatives. Managing complexity requires a structured approach, interdisciplinary collaboration, and robust project management practices to ensure comprehensive analysis and effective implementation of recommendations.

Balancing Cost and Value: Balancing cost reduction objectives with value enhancement goals can be challenging, especially when faced with conflicting priorities or trade-offs. Achieving the right balance requires careful consideration of project objectives, stakeholder requirements, and potential impacts on project outcomes to ensure that cost savings do not compromise project quality or performance.

Early Engagement: Engage stakeholders early in the Value Engineering process to ensure buy-in and alignment with project objectives. Solicit input from diverse perspectives to identify opportunities and challenges comprehensively.

Data-Driven Analysis: Conduct thorough data analysis and research to inform Value Engineering decisions. Utilize historical data, benchmarking studies, and industry best practices to support recommendations and validate cost-saving opportunities.

Cross-Functional Collaboration: Foster collaboration among multidisciplinary teams, including engineers, designers, procurement specialists, and end-users, to leverage diverse expertise and perspectives. Encourage open dialogue and knowledge sharing to generate innovative solutions and overcome challenges collaboratively.

Risk Management: Integrate risk management principles into Value Engineering initiatives to anticipate potential risks and mitigate their impacts on project outcomes. Conduct risk assessments, contingency planning, and scenario analysis to proactively address uncertainties and ensure project success.

Continuous Improvement: Embrace a culture of continuous improvement by evaluating and refining Value Engineering processes and practices based on lessons learned from past projects. Implement feedback mechanisms, performance metrics, and post-implementation reviews to track progress and identify opportunities for further optimization.

By acknowledging and addressing these challenges through best practices, organizations can enhance the effectiveness of Value Engineering initiatives, maximize cost savings, and optimize project outcomes. Through proactive stakeholder engagement, data-driven analysis, interdisciplinary collaboration, and continuous improvement, Value Engineering becomes a powerful tool for driving innovation, efficiency, and value creation across diverse projects and industries.

Integration with Cost Management

Value Engineering is intricately linked with cost management, both aiming to optimize project outcomes while minimizing expenses. This section explores the integration of Value Engineering with cost management practices, highlighting synergies and strategies for maximizing project value.

1. Cost Management Principles:

Cost management involves the systematic planning, monitoring, and controlling of project costs throughout the project lifecycle. It encompasses activities such as cost estimation, budgeting, tracking, and control, with the overarching goal of delivering projects within budgetary constraints while meeting quality and performance standards.

2. Synergies with Value Engineering:

Value Engineering complements cost management by providing a structured approach to identifying opportunities for cost optimization and value enhancement. While cost management focuses on controlling expenses and adhering to budget constraints, Value Engineering seeks to optimize project value by reevaluating project requirements, processes, and resources to achieve better outcomes at lower costs.

3. Incorporating Value Engineering into Cost Management Practices:

Integrating Value Engineering into cost management practices involves embedding Value Engineering principles and techniques into existing cost management processes. This may include conducting Value Engineering workshops during project planning stages, incorporating Value Engineering analyses into cost estimation and budgeting processes, and utilizing Value Engineering recommendations to inform cost control strategies.

4. Value-Based Decision Making:

By integrating Value Engineering into cost management practices, project teams can adopt a value-based approach to decision-making. This involves evaluating project alternatives based on their ability to maximize value while minimizing costs, rather than solely focusing on cost reduction. Value-based decision-making ensures that project investments align with project objectives and deliver optimal value for stakeholders.

5. Continuous Improvement:

Integration of Value Engineering with cost management promotes a culture of continuous improvement in project cost management practices. By leveraging Value Engineering techniques to identify cost-saving opportunities and value enhancement strategies, project teams can continuously refine and optimize their cost management processes, driving efficiency and maximizing project value over time.

The integration of Value Engineering with cost management practices offers a holistic approach to optimizing project outcomes and maximizing value for stakeholders. By embedding Value Engineering principles and techniques into cost management processes, project teams can identify opportunities for cost optimization, enhance project value, and achieve greater efficiency and effectiveness in managing project costs. Through synergistic collaboration and value-based decision-making, integration of Value Engineering with cost management becomes a cornerstone of project success, ensuring that projects deliver superior outcomes while remaining cost-effective and competitive in the marketplace.

Future Trends in Value Engineering

The landscape of Value Engineering is continuously evolving, driven by technological advancements, changing market dynamics, and evolving project requirements. In this section, we explore emerging trends and innovations shaping the future of Value Engineering.

1. Integration of Advanced Technologies:

The future of Value Engineering lies in the integration

of advanced technologies such as artificial intelligence (AI), machine learning (ML), and data analytics. These technologies enable more sophisticated analysis of project data, predictive modelling of cost-saving opportunities, and automated decision-making processes, enhancing the efficiency and effectiveness of Value Engineering initiatives.

2. Digitalization of Value Engineering Processes:

Digitalization is transforming Value Engineering processes, enabling remote collaboration, real-time data exchange, and virtual simulations. Digital tools and platforms facilitate more efficient communication among project stakeholders, streamline data collection and analysis, and enhance the visualization of project concepts and ideas, driving innovation and accelerating decision-making processes.

3. Sustainability Integration:

The integration of sustainability considerations into Value Engineering practices is emerging as a key trend. As organizations increasingly prioritize sustainability goals, Value Engineering will play a crucial role in identifying opportunities for reducing environmental impact, enhancing resource efficiency, and achieving sustainable development objectives while optimizing project costs and value.

4. Emphasis on Lifecycle Cost Analysis:

Future Value Engineering initiatives will place greater emphasis on lifecycle cost analysis, considering the total cost of ownership over the entire lifecycle of a project or asset. This holistic approach enables project teams to assess the long-term implications of design decisions, maintenance requirements, and operational costs, ensuring that projects deliver sustainable value over time.

5. Focus on Value-Based Innovation:

Future Value Engineering initiatives will increasingly focus on value-based innovation, prioritizing solutions that deliver the greatest value to stakeholders. This involves shifting from a purely cost-driven approach to one that emphasizes value creation, innovation, and customer-centricity, driving competitive advantage and market differentiation.

The future of Value Engineering holds immense promise, fuelled by technological advancements, sustainability imperatives, and evolving project requirements. By embracing emerging trends and innovations, organizations can leverage Value Engineering as a strategic tool for optimizing project outcomes, driving innovation, and delivering sustainable value in an increasingly complex and dynamic business environment.

Value Engineering stands as a cornerstone of modern project management, offering a systematic approach to optimizing value and minimizing costs across diverse industries and project types. As we conclude this exploration of Value Engineering, it's evident that its principles and practices are instrumental in driving innovation, efficiency, and value creation in today's dynamic business environment.

Throughout this chapter, we've delved into the foundational principles of Value Engineering, its applications across various industries, and the integration of Value Engineering with cost management practices. We've explored challenges and best practices, future trends, and the transformative potential of Value Engineering in shaping the future of project management.

Looking ahead, the future of Value Engineering holds immense promise, driven by technological advancements, sustainability imperatives, and a growing focus on value-based decision-making. By embracing emerging trends and innovations, organizations can leverage Value Engineering as a strategic tool for driving efficiency, innovation, and sustainable value creation in their projects.

As we navigate the complexities of an ever-evolving

business landscape, Value Engineering remains a guiding light, empowering organizations to optimize project outcomes, enhance stakeholder value, and achieve greater success in their endeavours. By embracing the principles of Value Engineering and fostering a culture of innovation and continuous improvement, we can unlock new opportunities, overcome challenges, and chart a course towards a future defined by excellence and success.

CHAPTER 6: CONTRACT MANAGEMENT AND COST

Introduction to Contract Management

Contract management plays a pivotal role in the realm of cost management, serving as a cornerstone for ensuring project success and financial efficiency. In this section, we delve into the fundamental importance of contract management and its direct impact on project costs and outcomes.

Overview of the Importance of Contract Management:

Contract management encompasses the entire lifecycle of contracts, from negotiation and drafting to execution and administration. At its core, it involves the effective management and oversight of contractual agreements between parties involved in a project. The significance of contract management lies in its ability to establish clear expectations, allocate responsibilities, and mitigate risks, all of which directly influence project costs and performance.

Contribution to Project Cost Control and Optimization:

Effective contract management is essential for controlling project costs and optimizing resource utilization. By defining the scope of work, terms, and conditions, contracts provide a framework for managing project expenses and ensuring adherence to budgetary constraints. Moreover, robust contract management practices enable proactive identification and mitigation of cost-related risks, such as scope changes, cost overruns, and disputes, thereby safeguarding project finances and ensuring cost-effective project delivery.

In essence, contract management serves as a linchpin for aligning project objectives, managing stakeholder expectations, and safeguarding project finances. Its effective implementation not only fosters transparency and accountability but also fosters trust and collaboration among project stakeholders, laying the groundwork for successful project outcomes and financial sustainability.

Types of Contracts

Contracts are the foundation of project engagements, dictating the terms, responsibilities, and financial obligations of parties involved. In this section, we explore the various types of contracts commonly used in project management and their implications for project costs and risk management.

Lump Sum Contracts:

Lump sum contracts, also known as fixed-price contracts, stipulate a predetermined sum for the completion of defined project deliverables.

Implications for Project Costs: Lump sum contracts provide cost certainty to project owners, as the total project cost is established upfront. However, contractors may inflate prices to mitigate risk, potentially resulting in higher initial costs.

Cost-Reimbursable Contracts:

Cost-reimbursable contracts reimburse the contractor for all legitimate project costs incurred, plus a fee or profit margin.

Implications for Project Costs: Cost-reimbursable contracts offer flexibility in project scope changes but may lead to cost overruns if not carefully managed. Project owners bear the risk of cost escalation, requiring robust cost tracking and control mechanisms.

Time and Material Contracts:

Time and material contracts involve paying the contractor based on the actual time spent and materials used, plus a markup for profit.

Implications for Project Costs: Time and material contracts offer flexibility in project scope and duration but pose risks of cost uncertainty and scope creep. Project owners must closely monitor costs and progress to prevent budget overruns.

Unit Price Contracts:

Unit price contracts establish prices for specific units of work or materials, with payment based on the quantity supplied.

Implications for Project Costs: Unit price contracts offer transparency and control over project costs, as payments are tied to actual quantities delivered. However, inaccurate quantity estimates can lead to cost discrepancies and disputes.

Each contract type presents unique advantages and challenges in terms of project cost management and risk mitigation.

- Lump sum contracts provide cost certainty but may incentivize contractors to cut corners to maximize profits.

- Cost-reimbursable contracts offer flexibility but require stringent cost control measures to prevent budget overruns.

- Time and material contracts provide agility but necessitate vigilant monitoring to ensure costs remain within budget.

- Unit price contracts offer transparency but require accurate quantity estimates to avoid cost discrepancies.

In summary, selecting the appropriate contract type is critical for aligning project objectives, managing costs, and mitigating risks effectively. Project stakeholders must carefully evaluate the implications of each contract type on project finances and implement robust contract management practices to ensure successful project outcomes.

Key Components of Contract Management

Contract management comprises a series of essential components that collectively ensure the effective execution and administration of contractual agreements. In this section, we delve into the critical elements of contract management, emphasizing their significance in controlling project costs and optimizing contractual outcomes.

1. Contract Negotiation:

Definition: Contract negotiation involves the process of reaching mutually acceptable terms and conditions between parties before contract execution.

Significance: Effective negotiation lays the foundation for a successful contractual relationship, defining project scope, deliverables, pricing, and timelines.

Cost Control Implications: Skilful negotiation can lead to favourable terms that mitigate cost risks and promote cost-effective project execution.

2. Contract Drafting:

Definition: Contract drafting entails the creation of a formal written document that reflects the terms and conditions agreed upon during negotiation.

Significance: A well-drafted contract provides clarity and certainty regarding project requirements, responsibilities, and obligations, reducing the likelihood of misunderstandings and disputes.

Cost Control Implications: Clear and comprehensive contract language helps prevent cost disputes and facilitates efficient cost management throughout the project lifecycle.

3. Contract Execution:

Definition: Contract execution involves the formal signing and acceptance of the contract by all parties, signalling the commencement of contractual obligations.

Significance: Execution confirms the parties' commitment to abide by the terms of the contract and initiates project implementation activities.

Cost Control Implications: Timely execution ensures project activities proceed as planned, minimizing delays and cost overruns associated with contractual uncertainty.

4. Contract Administration:

Definition: Contract administration encompasses the ongoing management and oversight of contractual performance, compliance, and documentation throughout the contract lifecycle.

Significance: Effective administration ensures adherence to contractual requirements, monitors project progress, and addresses issues as they arise, reducing the likelihood of cost overruns and disputes.

Cost Control Implications: Rigorous contract administration facilitates timely identification and resolution of cost-related issues, optimizing project cost management and financial performance.

5. Change Management:

Definition: Change management involves the systematic process of evaluating, approving, and implementing changes to the contract scope, specifications, or deliverables.

Significance: Proper change management controls scope creep, minimizes project disruptions, and preserves project cost and schedule integrity.

Cost Control Implications: Effective change management practices help prevent unauthorized changes, mitigate cost impacts, and ensure accurate cost tracking and forecasting.

6. Performance Monitoring:

Definition: Performance monitoring entails tracking and evaluating contractor performance against contractual requirements, quality standards, and key performance indicators (KPIs).

Significance: Monitoring performance enables early identification of deviations from the contract terms, allowing for timely corrective actions to mitigate cost and schedule impacts.

Cost Control Implications: Proactive performance monitoring safeguards project costs by identifying inefficiencies, deficiencies, or non-compliance issues that could lead to cost overruns or contractual disputes.

In essence, each component of contract management plays a vital role in safeguarding project costs, ensuring contractual compliance, and optimizing project outcomes. By prioritizing effective contract management practices, project stakeholders can mitigate cost risks, foster collaboration, and drive successful project delivery.

Cost Considerations in Contract Management

Cost considerations are integral to contract management, as they directly impact project budgets, financial performance, and overall project success. In this section, we explore the various cost-related factors that influence contract management decisions and practices.

1. Pricing Mechanisms:

Fixed Price vs. Cost-Reimbursable: Contract pricing mechanisms, such as fixed-price and cost-reimbursable contracts, have distinct cost implications. Fixed-price contracts provide cost certainty but may lead to increased risk for contractors, while cost-reimbursable contracts offer flexibility but require diligent cost tracking and control.

2. Cost Escalation Clauses:

Definition: Cost escalation clauses allow for adjustments to contract prices to account for changes in market conditions, labour rates, material costs, or other factors beyond the contractor's control.

Importance: Cost escalation clauses protect both parties from unforeseen cost increases, providing a mechanism for managing inflationary pressures and maintaining project profitability.

3. Change Order Management:

Scope Changes: Changes to project scope often result in additional costs or schedule adjustments. Effective change order management processes ensure that changes are properly documented, evaluated for cost impacts, and approved in accordance with contractual requirements.

Cost Tracking: Accurate cost tracking is essential for documenting changes, assessing their financial implications, and ensuring that costs remain within budgetary constraints.

4. Payment Terms and Schedule:

Milestone Payments: Contract payment terms and schedules dictate when and how payments are made to contractors based on project milestones or deliverables. Timely and accurate payments incentivize contractor performance and mitigate payment-related disputes.

Retention or Holdback: Retention or holdback provisions withhold a portion of payments until project completion or satisfactory performance. This ensures contractor accountability and provides recourse for addressing defects or deficiencies in workmanship.

5. Value Engineering and Cost Optimization:

Integration: Incorporating value engineering principles into contract management practices can lead to cost savings, performance improvements, and enhanced project value.

Opportunities: Contract management presents opportunities for identifying and implementing value engineering initiatives, such as redesigning project components or optimizing construction methods to reduce costs while maintaining or enhancing project quality.

6. Cost Reporting and Transparency:

Financial Reporting: Transparent and timely cost reporting is essential for monitoring project financial performance, tracking expenditures, and identifying variances against budgeted costs.

Contractual Obligations: Contractual obligations related to cost reporting and transparency ensure accountability and facilitate informed decision-making by project stakeholders.

In summary, cost considerations permeate every aspect of contract management, from contract negotiation and execution to performance monitoring and payment administration. By prioritizing cost-effective contract management practices and aligning contractual arrangements with project objectives, project stakeholders can optimize project costs, mitigate financial risks, and enhance project outcomes.

Risk Management in Contract Management

Risk management is a cornerstone of successful contract management, integral to ensuring project success and financial viability. It involves a systematic approach to identifying, assessing, and mitigating risks that could impact project costs, schedules, and outcomes. Here, we delve into the multifaceted nature of risk management in contract management and its profound implications for project cost control.

Contracts inherently contain risks stemming from ambiguities, incomplete scope definition, or unrealistic expectations. These risks can manifest as disputes, delays, or cost overruns if not professionally managed. Moreover, external factors such as market volatility, regulatory changes, or unforeseen events can introduce additional risks that must be addressed.

Risk assessment involves evaluating the probability and potential impact of identified risks on project objectives. Risks with high likelihood and significant impact on project costs or schedule are prioritized for mitigation efforts. Critical risks that could jeopardize project success receive special attention and proactive management strategies.

Effective risk mitigation strategies involve a combination of contractual protections, contingency planning, and proactive risk control measures. Contractual provisions, such as indemnification clauses or insurance requirements, allocate responsibility and provide safeguards against potential liabilities. Contingency plans and alternative strategies are developed to address unforeseen risks and minimize their impact on project costs and schedule.

Change management processes are integral to risk control, ensuring that changes to project scope or requirements are evaluated for their impact on costs and schedule. Proper change management procedures mitigate risks associated with scope changes by providing a structured approach to assessing, approving, and implementing changes while minimizing cost impacts.

Contractual disputes and claims can escalate project costs and disrupt project progress if not promptly addressed. Establishing effective dispute resolution mechanisms and claims management processes is crucial for minimizing the financial impact of disputes and ensuring timely resolution to avoid cost overruns and delays.

Monitoring contractor performance and compliance with contractual obligations is essential for identifying potential risks and performance issues early on. Quality assurance measures help mitigate the risk of rework or delays, ensuring that project costs remain within budgetary constraints.

Open communication and stakeholder engagement foster

transparency and collaboration, enabling proactive risk management efforts and timely resolution of issues. Regular reporting on risk status and mitigation efforts keeps stakeholders informed and facilitates informed decision-making to mitigate potential cost impacts.

In essence, effective risk management in contract management is vital for safeguarding project costs, protecting against potential losses, and ensuring project success. By adopting a proactive approach to risk identification, assessment, and mitigation, project stakeholders can minimize cost overruns, optimize project outcomes, and enhance stakeholder value.

Performance Measurement and Evaluation

Performance measurement and evaluation are critical components of effective contract management, providing a framework for assessing contractor performance, monitoring project progress, and ensuring adherence to contractual obligations. These processes are essential for managing costs, maintaining quality, and achieving project objectives. This section delves into the key elements of performance measurement and evaluation in contract management.

The foundation of performance measurement is the establishment of Key Performance Indicators (KPIs). These KPIs should be clearly defined, measurable, and aligned with project objectives and contractual requirements. Common KPIs in contract management include cost performance, schedule adherence, quality standards, and stakeholder satisfaction. By setting these benchmarks, project stakeholders can objectively assess performance and identify areas requiring attention.

Continuous monitoring of contractor performance against established KPIs is vital. This involves collecting relevant data, analysing performance trends, and comparing actual results to predefined targets. Regular performance tracking allows for early identification of issues, enabling timely corrective actions to prevent cost overruns and schedule delays. It also highlights contractor strengths and areas for potential improvement.

Performance evaluation extends beyond contractor performance to include overall project progress. This involves reviewing project documentation, conducting site inspections, and engaging with stakeholders to gauge progress against the project schedule and deliverables. Regular evaluations help ensure that the project is on track and that any deviations are promptly addressed.

A key aspect of performance measurement is analysing cost performance. This includes assessing budget variances, forecasting cost-to-complete, and conducting earned value analysis. These analyses provide insights into the project's financial health, highlighting any deviations from the budget and identifying opportunities for cost savings. Effective cost performance analysis helps maintain financial control and ensures that the project remains within budget.

Ensuring compliance with contractual specifications, quality standards, and regulatory requirements is a critical part of performance measurement. Quality assurance activities, such as inspections, audits, and quality control processes, verify that project deliverables meet established criteria. Maintaining high-quality standards minimizes the risk of rework, cost overruns, and delays.

Engaging stakeholders and soliciting their feedback on contractor performance fosters transparency and accountability. Regular communication channels, such as performance review meetings and feedback mechanisms, facilitate open dialogue and collaboration. Stakeholder feedback provides valuable insights into performance perceptions and areas for improvement, enhancing overall project satisfaction.

Performance measurement serves as a catalyst for continuous improvement initiatives. By analysing performance data and learning from evaluations, project stakeholders can implement process improvements, share best practices, and take corrective actions. Continuous improvement efforts lead to enhanced project performance, optimized resource utilization, and greater cost efficiencies.

Assessing compliance with contractual obligations, such as reporting requirements, deliverable schedules, and payment terms, ensures adherence to contract terms. Regular evaluations of contractual compliance help minimize the risk of disputes, penalties, and non-compliance issues, maintaining the integrity of the contract and protecting project interests.

In summary, performance measurement and evaluation are indispensable for effective contract management. They provide a structured approach to assessing contractor performance, monitoring project progress, and ensuring compliance with contractual obligations. By implementing robust performance measurement systems, project stakeholders can optimize project outcomes, control costs, and enhance overall project delivery.

Dispute Resolution and Claims Management

Dispute resolution and claims management are critical aspects of contract management, ensuring that disagreements are handled efficiently, and claims are managed effectively to minimize disruptions and maintain project progress. This section explores the strategies and practices essential for resolving disputes and managing claims in contract management.

Disputes and claims in contract management often arise from misunderstandings, differing interpretations of contract terms, delays, cost overruns, and quality issues. Understanding the common causes of disputes helps in proactively addressing potential conflicts and establishing a framework for effective resolution.

The best way to manage disputes is to prevent them from occurring. This involves clear and detailed contract drafting, precise scope definition, transparent communication, and regular progress reviews. By setting clear expectations and fostering open dialogue among stakeholders, potential issues can be identified and resolved before they escalate into formal disputes.

Dispute Resolution Mechanisms:

Contracts typically outline specific mechanisms for resolving disputes, including negotiation, mediation, arbitration, and litigation. Each method has its advantages and appropriate applications:

Negotiation: The first step in dispute resolution, where parties attempt to resolve the issue amicably without third-party intervention. Effective negotiation relies on open communication, mutual understanding, and a willingness to compromise.

Mediation: Involves a neutral third party who facilitates discussions between disputing parties to help them reach a mutually acceptable solution. Mediation is less formal than arbitration and litigation and often quicker and more cost-effective.

Arbitration: A more formal process where an arbitrator or panel makes a binding decision on the dispute. Arbitration can be faster and less expensive than litigation, but it still provides a structured resolution framework.

Litigation: The last resort, involving a formal court process. Litigation is usually time-consuming and costly, and it is used when other methods fail or when a binding legal judgment is necessary.

Effective Claims Management:

Claims management involves systematically handling claims for additional time or compensation due to changes, delays, or unforeseen circumstances. Key steps in effective claims management include:

Documentation: Maintaining detailed records of all project activities, communications, and changes. Comprehensive documentation is crucial for supporting claims and demonstrating compliance with contractual obligations.

Timely Notification: Promptly notifying relevant parties of potential claims as they arise. This allows for early assessment and resolution of claims, preventing escalation.

Detailed Claim Submissions: Preparing detailed and well-supported claims submissions that outline the basis for the claim, the impact on the project, and the requested compensation or extension. Clear and concise submissions facilitate faster and fairer resolutions.

Collaborative Resolution: Engaging in open discussions with stakeholders to explore potential solutions and reach agreements on claims. Collaborative resolution fosters a cooperative atmosphere and can lead to more amicable outcomes.

Dispute and Claims Resolution Strategies:

Successful dispute and claims resolution require strategic planning and execution. Some effective strategies include:

Early Intervention: Addressing disputes and claims early to prevent them from escalating. Early intervention allows for more options and lessens the impact on project progress and costs.

Expert Involvement: Engaging experts, such as legal advisors or claims specialists, to provide insights and support in complex disputes or claims. Expert involvement ensures that resolutions are based on sound analysis and legal principles.

Structured Process: Implementing a structured process for managing disputes and claims, including clear procedures, timelines, and responsibilities. A structured process ensures consistency and transparency in handling disputes and claims.

Finally, learning from past disputes and claims is essential for improving future contract management practices. Analysing the root causes of disputes, understanding the effectiveness of resolution strategies, and incorporating lessons learned into future contracts can help mitigate risks and enhance overall project management.

In conclusion, effective dispute resolution and claims management are vital for maintaining project momentum, controlling costs, and ensuring successful project delivery. By adopting proactive prevention measures, utilizing appropriate resolution mechanisms, and implementing strategic claims management practices, project stakeholders can navigate disputes and claims efficiently and maintain positive working relationships.

Compliance and Ethics in Contract Management

Compliance and ethics are foundational elements of effective contract management, ensuring that all parties adhere to legal standards, contractual obligations, and ethical principles. In this section, we delve into the significance of compliance and ethics in contract management, exploring best practices, common challenges, and the benefits of maintaining high ethical standards.

Compliance involves adhering to laws, regulations, and contractual terms, while ethics pertains to conducting business with integrity, fairness, and transparency. Both are crucial for fostering trust, minimizing legal risks, and ensuring long-term project success. Adhering to compliance and ethics standards helps organizations avoid legal penalties, safeguard their reputations, and build strong stakeholder relationships.

Organizations should develop and enforce comprehensive ethical guidelines that outline expected behaviours and practices in contract management. These guidelines should cover aspects such as conflict of interest, confidentiality, fair dealing, and responsible communication. By clearly defining ethical standards, organizations can create a culture of integrity and accountability.

Legal compliance in contract management involves understanding and adhering to relevant laws, regulations, and industry standards. This includes labour laws, environmental regulations, health and safety standards, and financial reporting requirements. Organizations should regularly review and update their compliance policies to reflect changes in legislation and industry practices.

Training and awareness programs are essential for educating employees and contractors about compliance and ethics. These programs should cover legal requirements, ethical guidelines, and best practices in contract management. Regular training helps ensure that all parties understand their responsibilities and are equipped to handle ethical dilemmas appropriately.

Effective compliance monitoring involves implementing systems and processes to track adherence to legal and ethical standards. This includes regular audits, compliance reviews, and performance evaluations. Monitoring systems should identify potential compliance issues early and provide mechanisms for corrective actions.

Ethical dilemmas in contract management can arise from conflicts of interest, unfair practices, or pressure to compromise standards for short-term gains. Organizations should establish clear procedures for reporting and addressing ethical concerns. Encouraging an open-door policy and protecting whistleblowers can help create a safe environment for raising ethical issues.

Transparency in contract management involves clear and open communication about project activities, decisions, and performance. Accountability requires that all parties take responsibility for their actions and decisions. Together, transparency and accountability help build trust among stakeholders and ensure that projects are managed ethically.

Fostering a culture of integrity involves integrating ethical principles into every aspect of contract management. Leadership should model ethical behaviour and reinforce the importance of ethics through policies, rewards, and recognition programs. A culture of integrity supports ethical decision-making and helps prevent misconduct.

When non-compliance or ethical breaches occur, organizations must respond promptly and effectively. This involves conducting thorough investigations, taking disciplinary actions when necessary, and implementing measures to prevent future occurrences. Addressing breaches transparently demonstrates a commitment to ethical standards and deters future violations.

Maintaining high standards of compliance and ethics in contract management offers numerous benefits. It enhances the organization's reputation, reduces the risk of legal penalties, and fosters strong relationships with clients, contractors, and stakeholders. Ethical contract management also contributes to sustainable business practices and long-term success.

Examining case studies and best practices provides valuable insights into effective compliance and ethics management. Learning from real-world examples helps organizations understand the challenges and strategies involved in upholding ethical standards in contract management.

In conclusion, compliance and ethics are essential for successful contract management. By establishing clear ethical guidelines, ensuring legal compliance, providing training, and promoting a culture of integrity, organizations can navigate complex contractual landscapes with confidence. Upholding high standards of compliance and ethics not only protects organizations from legal and reputational risks but also contributes to building a sustainable and responsible business environment.

Technology and Innovation in Contract Management

In the ever-evolving landscape of contract management, technology and innovation play pivotal roles in streamlining processes, enhancing accuracy, and driving efficiency. This section explores the transformative impact of technological advancements and innovative practices on contract management, offering insights into the tools and methodologies that are reshaping the field.

Digital transformation in contract management involves the adoption of advanced technologies to automate, streamline, and improve various aspects of the contract lifecycle. This shift from manual, paper-based processes to digital solutions enhances efficiency, reduces errors, and facilitates better collaboration among stakeholders.

Contract Lifecycle Management (CLM) software is a cornerstone of modern contract management. CLM platforms provide comprehensive solutions for drafting, reviewing, approving, storing, and managing contracts. These tools offer functionalities such as automated workflows, version control, electronic signatures, and real-time collaboration, significantly reducing administrative burdens and accelerating contract processing times.

AI and ML technologies are revolutionizing contract management by enabling advanced data analysis, predictive analytics, and automation. AI-powered tools can automatically extract and analyse key contract terms, identify risks, and suggest optimal clauses based on historical data. Machine learning algorithms can predict potential contract performance issues, enabling proactive risk management and decision-making.

Blockchain technology introduces the concept of smart contracts, which are self-executing contracts with the terms directly written into code. Smart contracts automatically enforce the terms and conditions of an agreement, reducing the need for intermediaries and minimizing the risk of disputes. Blockchain's transparency and immutability also enhance contract security and trust among parties.

Cloud-based contract management solutions offer scalability, flexibility, and accessibility. These platforms enable remote access to contract data, support real-time updates, and facilitate collaboration across geographically dispersed teams. Cloud storage also ensures data security and disaster recovery, protecting critical contract information.

Integrating contract management systems with other enterprise software, such as Enterprise Resource Planning (ERP), Customer Relationship Management (CRM), and procurement systems, enhances data consistency and operational efficiency. Seamless integration allows for better visibility into contract-related data, improving decision-making and alignment with overall business processes.

Advanced data analytics tools provide valuable insights into contract performance, compliance, and financial impact. Dashboards and reporting features enable stakeholders to monitor key metrics, identify trends, and make data-driven decisions. Analytics also help in identifying bottlenecks and areas for improvement, supporting continuous optimization of contract management practices.

Mobile applications for contract management offer on-the-go access to contract data, enabling users to review, approve, and manage contracts from their smartphones or tablets. This mobility enhances productivity and responsiveness, especially for professionals who frequently travel or work remotely.

Technology enhances contract security through advanced encryption, multi-factor authentication, and secure access controls. These measures protect sensitive contract information from unauthorized access and cyber threats, ensuring data integrity and confidentiality.

Collaboration tools such as virtual meeting platforms, shared workspaces, and collaborative editing features facilitate seamless communication and teamwork among stakeholders. These tools enhance coordination, reduce misunderstandings, and expedite the contract negotiation and approval process.

Despite the benefits, adopting new technologies in contract

management also presents challenges, such as the initial investment cost, integration complexities, and the need for staff training. Organizations must carefully evaluate their specific needs, choose the right solutions, and plan for a smooth implementation process.

Looking ahead, emerging technologies such as quantum computing, advanced AI, and Internet of Things (IoT) integration hold the potential to further revolutionize contract management. Staying abreast of these trends and continuously exploring innovative solutions will be crucial for organizations aiming to maintain a competitive edge.

In conclusion, technology and innovation are driving profound changes in contract management, enhancing efficiency, accuracy, and collaboration. By embracing digital transformation, leveraging advanced tools, and staying informed about emerging trends, organizations can optimize their contract management practices, reduce risks, and achieve greater operational excellence.

Challenges and Best Practices

Contract management is a complex discipline that requires addressing various challenges to ensure successful outcomes. This section delves into the common challenges faced in contract management and outlines best practices to overcome these obstacles, ensuring effective and efficient management of contracts.

Challenges in Contract Management

One of the primary challenges is managing the complexity and volume of contracts. Contracts often contain numerous clauses, stipulations, and dependencies that require meticulous tracking and management. The complexity increases with multi-party agreements and international contracts, where legal requirements and business norms vary significantly.

Compliance and regulatory issues present another significant challenge. Adhering to various legal and regulatory requirements is critical but challenging. Non-compliance can lead to substantial legal and financial repercussions. Keeping abreast of changing regulations and ensuring compliance across all contracts demands continuous effort and vigilance.

Inefficient processes and manual handling of contracts are time-consuming and prone to errors. Relying on manual processes for contract creation, approval, and management can lead to delays, missed deadlines, and increased costs, impacting overall project efficiency.

Risk management is a crucial yet challenging aspect of contract management. Identifying, assessing, and mitigating risks associated with contracts is essential to prevent disputes, financial losses, and project delays. Contracts often contain hidden risks that, if not responsibly managed, can lead to significant issues.

Effective communication and collaboration among stakeholders are vital for successful contract management. Poor communication can result in misunderstandings, misaligned expectations, and conflicts, all of which can jeopardize the success of a contract.

Protecting sensitive contract information from unauthorized access and cyber threats is paramount. Ensuring data security and confidentiality while maintaining accessibility for authorized personnel is a delicate balance that must be achieved to safeguard contract information.

Best Practices in Contract Management

To address these challenges, implementing robust contract management systems is essential. Adopting a comprehensive Contract Lifecycle Management (CLM) system can streamline and automate contract processes. CLM systems provide features such as automated workflows, version control, electronic signatures, and real-time collaboration, reducing administrative burdens and enhancing efficiency.

Standardizing contract templates and processes can help ensure consistency, reduce errors, and save time. Developing standardized templates that include commonly used clauses and regularly updating them to reflect legal and regulatory changes can significantly improve contract management practices.

Conducting regular compliance audits is a proactive approach to identifying and rectifying non-compliance issues early. These audits should assess adherence to legal requirements, regulatory standards, and internal policies, ensuring that contracts align with all relevant laws and guidelines.

Enhancing risk management practices is critical. This involves identifying potential risks during the contract drafting phase, conducting thorough risk assessments, and developing mitigation strategies. Regularly reviewing and updating risk management plans ensures that emerging risks are addressed promptly.

Fostering effective communication and collaboration among all stakeholders is key. Utilizing collaborative tools and platforms can facilitate better coordination, ensuring that all parties are on the same page and working towards common goals. Encouraging open communication helps prevent misunderstandings and conflicts.

Investing in training and development for contract management professionals ensures they are equipped with the latest knowledge and skills. Providing ongoing training that covers legal and regulatory updates, best practices, and the use of contract management software can enhance overall contract management capabilities.

Ensuring data security and confidentiality is crucial. Implementing robust security measures such as encryption, multi-factor authentication, and access controls can protect sensitive contract data. Regular security audits and updates help safeguard information against cyber threats and unauthorized access.

Leveraging data analytics can provide valuable insights into contract performance, compliance, and financial impact. Utilizing data-driven decision-making helps identify trends, optimize processes, and improve overall contract management effectiveness.

Regularly monitoring and evaluating contract performance ensures that objectives are being met and areas for improvement are identified. Performance metrics should include key indicators such as compliance rates, cycle times, cost savings, and risk mitigation effectiveness.

Embracing continuous improvement is essential in contract management. Encouraging feedback, learning from past experiences, and staying updated on industry trends and best practices helps organizations refine their contract management processes and achieve better outcomes.

Navigating the challenges of contract management requires a strategic approach that combines robust systems, standardized processes, effective risk management, and continuous improvement. By implementing these best practices, organizations can enhance efficiency, ensure compliance, mitigate risks, and achieve successful contract outcomes. Embracing technology and fostering a culture of collaboration and innovation will further strengthen contract management capabilities, driving long-term business success.

In the dynamic realm of contract management, the ability to balance cost considerations with efficient contract execution is crucial. Effective contract management directly impacts an organization's bottom line, influencing not only immediate project outcomes but also long-term financial health and operational success. This concluding section synthesizes the key insights discussed in this chapter, emphasizing the importance of strategic contract management in achieving cost efficiency and risk mitigation.

Contract management serves as the backbone of successful project execution, ensuring that all parties fulfil their obligations while maintaining financial discipline. Understanding the types of contracts and their specific applications allows organizations to choose the most appropriate agreements for their needs. By leveraging the right contract type, companies can align contractual terms with their strategic goals, optimizing both performance and cost efficiency.

Key components of contract management, such as clear scope definition, detailed terms and conditions, and robust compliance measures, form the foundation of effective contracts. Addressing cost considerations from the outset ensures that financial constraints are respected throughout the contract lifecycle. Integrating risk management into contract planning further safeguards against unforeseen events that could escalate costs or disrupt project timelines.

Performance measurement and evaluation are critical for maintaining accountability and transparency in contract execution. Regular monitoring of contract performance helps identify areas for improvement and ensures that projects stay on track financially. When disputes arise, having a structured approach to dispute resolution and claims management minimizes disruptions and preserves relationships between contracting parties.

Ethical considerations and compliance with legal standards underpin the integrity of contract management practices. Adhering to ethical guidelines and regulatory requirements not only prevents legal complications but also builds trust with stakeholders. As technology continues to evolve, innovations in contract management tools offer new opportunities for efficiency and accuracy, making it essential for organizations to stay abreast of technological advancements.

Implementing best practices in contract management involves a commitment to continuous improvement. Organizations must learn from past experiences, adapt to changing conditions, and foster a culture of collaboration and communication. By addressing challenges head-on and adopting proactive strategies, companies can enhance their contract management capabilities, ultimately achieving better financial outcomes and project success.

In summary, effective contract management is a multifaceted discipline that integrates cost control, risk management, performance monitoring, and ethical practices. By adopting a strategic approach and leveraging modern tools and techniques, organizations can navigate the complexities of contract management, ensuring that contracts are executed efficiently and cost-effectively. As we move forward, the principles and best practices outlined in this chapter will serve as a guide for managing contracts in a way that aligns with organizational goals and promotes long-term success.

CHAPTER 7: COST REPORTING AND COMMUNICATION

Introduction to Cost Reporting and Communication

Effective cost reporting and communication are fundamental to successful project management. These practices ensure that all stakeholders have access to timely, accurate, and relevant financial information, enabling informed decision-making and fostering accountability. This section provides an overview of the significance of cost reporting and the crucial role of communication in managing project costs.

Cost reporting serves as the backbone of financial transparency within a project. It involves the systematic collection, analysis, and dissemination of cost-related data, offering a clear picture of the project's financial health at any given time. Regular and structured cost reporting helps project managers track expenditures, compare actual costs against budgeted figures, and identify any variances. This proactive approach allows for timely corrective actions, preventing minor issues from escalating into major financial problems.

Communication, on the other hand, is the conduit through which cost information flows to various stakeholders. Effective communication ensures that everyone involved in the project, from team members to senior executives and external partners, is kept informed about the project's financial status.

This transparency builds trust and aligns the team towards common financial objectives. Clear, concise, and consistent communication helps in setting expectations, reducing misunderstandings, and facilitating collaboration.

Together, cost reporting and communication form a robust framework for managing project finances. They enable stakeholders to monitor progress, assess risks, and make decisions based on accurate and up-to-date information. In today's fast-paced project environments, the ability to quickly disseminate financial insights and adapt to changing circumstances is a critical success factor. Therefore, mastering the art of cost reporting and communication is essential for any project manager aiming to deliver projects within budget and on time.

In summary, the introduction to cost reporting and communication highlights their vital role in project management. These practices ensure financial transparency, foster accountability, and facilitate informed decision-making, all of which are crucial for achieving project success. As we delve deeper into this chapter, we will explore the various types of cost reports, essential elements of effective reporting, and best practices for communicating cost information to stakeholders.

Objectives of Cost Reporting

Cost reporting serves as a critical function in project management, providing a structured approach to track, analyse, and communicate financial information. Understanding the objectives of cost reporting helps in appreciating its value and integrating it effectively into project management practices. This section delves into the primary objectives of cost reporting and how they contribute to successful project execution.

One of the foremost objectives of cost reporting is to ensure transparency and accountability in project finances. Transparent cost reporting allows stakeholders to see where funds are being allocated and how they are being utilized.

This openness builds trust among stakeholders, including project sponsors, clients, and team members. It also holds project managers accountable for financial decisions, promoting responsible management of project resources.

Accurate and timely financial information is crucial for effective project management. Cost reports deliver up-to-date financial data, enabling project managers and stakeholders to make informed decisions. Timeliness ensures that potential issues are identified and addressed promptly, minimizing the risk of budget overruns and project delays. Accurate reporting prevents misallocation of resources and helps maintain financial integrity throughout the project lifecycle.

Cost reports are essential tools for decision-making. They provide a detailed view of the project's financial status, including actual costs, budget variances, and forecasted expenditures. This information is invaluable for assessing the financial health of the project and determining the need for adjustments. Informed decision-making, supported by comprehensive cost reports, helps in optimizing resource allocation, controlling costs, and achieving project objectives efficiently.

Cost reporting enables continuous monitoring of project progress and performance against the budget. By comparing actual expenditures with planned budgets, project managers can gauge whether the project is on track financially. Regular monitoring helps in identifying variances and understanding their causes. This ongoing assessment is crucial for maintaining control over project finances and ensuring that the project stays within its financial constraints.

Strategic planning and forecasting are integral to successful project management. Cost reports provide the historical data needed for accurate forecasting and strategic planning. By analysing past performance, project managers can predict future financial trends and make informed projections. This foresight aids in developing realistic budgets and financial plans, enhancing the overall strategic management of the project.

Effective communication of financial information is a key objective of cost reporting. Clear and concise cost reports facilitate better communication with stakeholders, ensuring that everyone is aware of the project's financial status. This shared understanding promotes alignment and cooperation among stakeholders, reducing the likelihood of conflicts and misunderstandings. Enhanced communication fosters a collaborative environment, contributing to the project's success.

The objectives of cost reporting extend beyond mere documentation of financial transactions. They encompass ensuring transparency and accountability, providing timely and accurate financial information, facilitating informed decision-making, monitoring progress and performance, supporting strategic planning, and forecasting, and enhancing communication with stakeholders. Achieving these objectives requires a systematic approach to cost reporting, integrating it seamlessly into the overall project management process. As we progress through this chapter, we will explore the various types of cost reports, key elements of effective reporting, and strategies for communicating financial information effectively.

Types of Cost Reports

Effective cost management relies heavily on the ability to produce and interpret various types of cost reports. Each type of report serves a specific purpose and provides different insights into the project's financial health. Understanding these reports enables project managers and stakeholders to make well-informed decisions. This section explores the primary types of cost reports used in project management.

Progress reports are essential for tracking the ongoing status of a project. They provide a snapshot of the project's current financial situation, highlighting actual costs incurred to date compared to the planned budget. These reports typically include information on completed tasks, remaining work, and any variances between actual and planned expenditures. Progress reports are crucial for identifying trends and making timely adjustments to keep the project on track.

Variance reports focus on the differences between budgeted and actual costs. They detail the variances for each cost item, explaining why these differences occurred and assessing their impact on the overall project budget. By pinpointing the sources of variances, project managers can investigate underlying issues, such as scope changes, inefficiencies, or unforeseen challenges. Addressing these variances promptly helps maintain financial control and project alignment.

Forecasting reports are forward-looking documents that project future financial performance based on current data and trends. These reports estimate the costs expected to be incurred until project completion, providing insights into whether the project is likely to stay within budget. Forecasting reports are invaluable for proactive financial planning, allowing project managers to anticipate potential cost overruns and adjust resource allocations accordingly.

Executive summaries are concise reports designed for senior management and stakeholders who need a high-level overview of the project's financial status. These summaries highlight key financial metrics, significant variances, and critical issues without delving into the detailed data. By presenting essential information in an accessible format, executive summaries facilitate quick decision-making and strategic planning.

Different stakeholders have varied information needs, and **customized reports** address these specific requirements. For example, a report for the finance team might focus on detailed budget breakdowns and financial analysis, while a report for the project team might emphasize task completion and resource utilization. Tailoring reports to the audience ensures that relevant and actionable information is communicated effectively.

Earned Value Management (EVM) reports integrate scope, schedule, and cost data to provide a comprehensive view of project performance. These reports use key metrics such as Cost Performance Index (CPI) and Schedule Performance Index (SPI) to assess project health. EVM reports are particularly useful for tracking project progress in relation to the planned budget and schedule, offering a balanced perspective on performance.

Cash flow reports track the flow of cash into and out of the project over time. They provide insights into liquidity and the timing of expenditures and receipts. Understanding cash flow is critical for ensuring that the project has sufficient funds to meet its financial obligations at any given time. Cash flow reports help project managers plan for upcoming financial needs and avoid cash shortages.

Ad hoc reports are generated on an as-needed basis to address specific questions or issues that arise during the project. These reports are flexible and can be tailored to focus on any aspect of the project's finances. Ad hoc reports are useful for in-depth analysis and troubleshooting, providing detailed insights that standard reports might not cover.

Each type of cost report plays a distinct role in managing project finances. Progress reports track ongoing status, variance reports identify discrepancies, forecasting reports project future costs, and executive summaries provide high-level overviews. Customized reports cater to specific stakeholder needs, while EVM reports offer a holistic view of project performance. Cash flow reports ensure liquidity, and ad hoc reports address unique concerns. Together, these reports form a comprehensive framework for effective cost management, enabling project managers to maintain control, make informed decisions, and achieve project success. As we move forward in this chapter, we will delve into the key elements of effective cost reports and the best practices for communicating financial information.

Key Elements of Effective Cost Reports

Creating effective cost reports is essential for maintaining control over project finances and ensuring that stakeholders are well-informed. Effective cost reports share several key elements that make them comprehensive, clear, and actionable. This section explores these elements in detail.

The foundation of any effective cost report is the accuracy and precision of the data it contains. Accurate reports reflect the true financial status of the project, while precision ensures that the data is detailed and specific enough to be useful. To achieve this, project managers must implement rigorous data collection and validation processes. Errors or inaccuracies in cost reports can lead to poor decision-making and jeopardize the project's financial health.

Timely reporting is crucial for proactive cost management. Regular updates allow project managers to quickly identify and address any financial issues before they escalate. Timeliness ensures that stakeholders are always working with the most current information, which is essential for making informed decisions. Establishing a consistent reporting schedule helps maintain discipline and ensures that everyone involved is kept up to date.

Cost reports should be clear and concise, presenting information in an easily digestible format. Avoiding jargon and using straightforward language helps ensure that all stakeholders, regardless of their financial expertise, can understand the report. Visual aids such as charts, graphs, and tables can enhance clarity by summarizing complex data in an accessible way. Clarity in reporting prevents misunderstandings and ensures that the key messages are conveyed effectively.

Effective cost reports focus on relevant information that stakeholders need to make decisions. This means including data that reflects the project's current status, highlights critical issues, and provides actionable insights. Irrelevant details can clutter the report and distract from the important points. Tailoring the content to the specific needs of the audience enhances the report's usefulness and impact.

While reports should be concise, they also need to provide comprehensive coverage of all significant cost aspects of the project. This includes actual costs, budgeted costs, variances, forecasts, and any potential risks or issues. Comprehensive reports enable a thorough understanding of the project's financial health and facilitate effective planning and control.

Consistency in cost reporting involves using standard formats, terminology, and metrics across all reports. This makes it easier to compare data over time and across different parts of the project. Consistent reporting practices also help stakeholders become familiar with the format, making it easier for them to interpret the information. Establishing standardized templates and guidelines can promote consistency.

Beyond merely presenting data, effective cost reports should provide actionable insights. This involves analysing the data to identify trends, potential issues, and opportunities for improvement. Reports should include recommendations based on the analysis, helping stakeholders understand the implications of the data and what steps should be taken next. Actionable insights drive proactive management and continuous improvement.

Transparency is vital for building trust among stakeholders. Cost reports should openly disclose all relevant financial information, including any assumptions, methodologies, and potential limitations. This transparency fosters an environment of accountability, where project managers and team members are responsible for the financial decisions and outcomes. Transparent reporting builds confidence and supports collaborative decision-making.

Different stakeholders have different information needs, and effective cost reports should be customized to address these needs. For example, executive summaries might focus on high-level financial health, while detailed reports for the finance team might delve into specific cost categories and variances. Customization ensures that each stakeholder receives the information they need in a format that is most useful to them.

Cost reports should be integrated with other project management reports, such as schedule and performance reports, to provide a holistic view of the project. This integration allows for a more comprehensive analysis and helps identify correlations between different project aspects. For instance, cost overruns might be linked to schedule delays, and understanding these connections can lead to more effective problem-solving.

Effective cost reports are characterized by their accuracy, timeliness, clarity, relevance, and comprehensive coverage. Consistency in format and terminology, actionable insights, transparency, customization for stakeholders, and integration with other project reports further enhance their value. By incorporating these key elements, project managers can create cost reports that not only inform but also drive proactive and informed decision-making. As we continue through this chapter, we will explore best practices for communicating cost information and ensuring that all stakeholders effectively utilize reports.

Cost Reporting Tools and Software

In the realm of cost management, the use of advanced tools and software has become indispensable. These technologies streamline the process of data collection, analysis, and reporting, enabling project managers to maintain accurate and up-to-date cost information. This section explores the various tools and software available for cost reporting, highlighting their features, benefits, and best practices for implementation.

Integrated project management software solutions, such as Microsoft Project, Primavera P6, and Oracle's Primavera Unifier, offer comprehensive platforms that combine scheduling, resource management, and cost control. These tools enable seamless integration of cost data with other project management functions, providing a holistic view of the project's performance.

- **Features:** Integrated solutions typically include budget tracking, forecasting, variance analysis, and earned value management (EVM) capabilities. They also offer customizable dashboards and reporting features.

- **Benefits:** By consolidating project data into a single platform, these tools enhance data accuracy and facilitate better communication among project teams. They support real-time updates and collaborative planning, which are essential for effective cost management.

Dedicated cost management software, such as CostX, Procore, and Sage 300 Construction and Real Estate, focuses specifically on cost estimation, tracking, and reporting. These tools are designed to handle the intricacies of cost management with specialized features.

- **Features:** These software solutions offer detailed cost estimation modules, bid management, cost forecasting, budget reconciliation, and change order management. They often include robust reporting capabilities with customizable templates and formats.

- **Benefits:** Specialized cost management software provides deep insights into cost-related aspects of the project, enhancing precision in budget planning and control. They are particularly useful for complex projects with extensive cost data to manage.

Cloud-based solutions, such as CoConstruct, Buildertrend, and Zoho Projects, offer flexibility and accessibility, enabling project teams to access cost data and reports from anywhere with an internet connection. These tools support remote collaboration and real-time updates.

- **Features:** Cloud-based platforms offer cost tracking, budget management, invoicing, and expense management. They often integrate with other cloud services, such as document storage and communication tools.
- **Benefits:** The primary advantage of cloud-based solutions is their accessibility and ease of use. They reduce the need for on-premises infrastructure and support scalability, making them ideal for growing businesses and dispersed teams.

Business Intelligence (BI) tools, such as Tableau, Power BI, and Qlik, enable advanced data analysis and visualization. These tools are used to create interactive and visually appealing reports that enhance the understanding of cost data.

- **Features:** BI tools offer powerful data analytics, visualization capabilities, dashboard creation, and integration with multiple data sources. They support drill-down analysis and predictive analytics.
- **Benefits:** By transforming raw data into insightful visualizations, BI tools help project managers and stakeholders quickly grasp complex cost information. They facilitate data-driven decision-making and uncover trends that might not be immediately apparent from traditional reports.

While advanced software solutions offer numerous advantages, spreadsheets, such as Microsoft Excel and Google Sheets, remain a staple for cost reporting due to their flexibility and familiarity.

- **Features:** Spreadsheets can be customized to suit specific reporting needs, with features such as formulas, pivot tables, charts, and macros. Pre-designed templates for cost reporting are widely available.
- **Benefits:** Spreadsheets are highly adaptable and can be tailored to fit unique project requirements. They are cost-effective and accessible, making them a practical choice for smaller projects or organizations with limited budgets.

Best Practices for Implementing Cost Reporting Tools

Selecting the right cost reporting tools and software is crucial for effective cost management. Here are some best practices for implementation:

1. **Assess Needs and Requirements:** Understand the specific needs of your project and organization. Consider factors such as project size, complexity, budget, and the level of detail required in cost reports.

2. **Evaluate Features and Integration:** Choose tools that offer the necessary features and integrate well with your existing project management systems. Look for software that supports real-time updates, collaborative features, and customizable reporting.

3. **User Training and Support:** Ensure that your team is adequately trained to use the selected tools. Comprehensive training and ongoing support are essential for maximizing the benefits of cost reporting software.

4. **Data Security and Accessibility:** Prioritize tools that offer robust data security measures, especially if dealing with sensitive financial information. Cloud-based solutions should provide secure access controls and encryption.

5. **Regular Updates and Maintenance:** Keep your software updated to benefit from the latest features and security enhancements. Regular maintenance ensures the continued reliability and performance of the tools.

6. **Feedback and Continuous Improvement:** Encourage feedback from users to identify areas for improvement. Continuously refine your cost reporting processes and tools to enhance accuracy and efficiency.

The use of advanced tools and software is pivotal in modern cost management. Integrated project management software, dedicated cost management solutions, cloud-based platforms, BI tools, and traditional spreadsheets each offer unique features and benefits. By selecting the right tools and implementing best practices, project managers can enhance the accuracy, efficiency, and effectiveness of cost reporting. This, in turn, supports informed decision-making and contributes to the overall success of the project. As we move forward, we will explore the best practices for communicating cost information to ensure that all stakeholders effectively utilize reports.

Developing a Cost Reporting Framework

Creating a robust cost reporting framework is essential for ensuring that all stakeholders have access to accurate, timely, and relevant cost information. A well-designed framework not only standardizes the process of cost reporting but also enhances the transparency and accountability of project financials. In this section, we will explore the key components and steps involved in developing an effective cost reporting framework.

1. Establishing Objectives and Requirements

The first step in developing a cost reporting framework is to clearly define the objectives and requirements of the cost reports. This involves identifying the specific information needs of different stakeholders, such as project managers, financial analysts, senior management, and external auditors. Understanding these requirements helps in designing reports that provide meaningful insights and support decision-making processes.

Key Considerations:

- **Stakeholder Needs:** Identify who will use the cost reports and what information they need.
- **Report Frequency:** Determine how often cost reports should be generated (e.g., weekly, monthly, quarterly).
- **Level of Detail:** Decide on the granularity of the cost data (e.g., overall project costs vs. detailed cost breakdowns).

2. Defining Cost Categories and Structures

A clear categorization of costs is crucial for effective cost reporting. This involves creating a cost structure that organizes expenses into predefined categories, such as labour, materials, equipment, overheads, and contingencies. A standardized cost structure facilitates consistent reporting and comparison across different projects.

Steps to Define Cost Structures:

•	**Identify Major Cost Categories:** Break down the project costs into broad categories.

•	**Subcategories:** Further divide each major category into more specific subcategories.

•	**Coding System:** Develop a coding system to uniquely identify each cost category and subcategory.

3. Implementing Data Collection and Integration Processes

Accurate cost reporting depends on reliable data collection and integration processes. This involves establishing procedures for gathering cost data from various sources, such as purchase orders, invoices, payroll records, and subcontractor reports. Integrating this data into a central system ensures that all relevant information is captured and readily available for reporting.

Best Practices:

•	**Automated Data Collection:** Use technology to automate data collection where possible, reducing manual entry errors.

•	**Data Validation:** Implement validation checks to ensure the accuracy and completeness of the data.

•	**Integration:** Ensure seamless integration of data from various systems (e.g., accounting software, project management tools).

4. Designing Report Templates and Dashboards

Effective cost reporting frameworks include standardized report templates and dashboards that present cost information in a clear and accessible format. Templates should be designed to highlight key metrics, trends, and variances, enabling stakeholders to quickly grasp the financial status of the project.

Design Tips:

- **Consistency:** Use consistent formatting and terminology across all reports.
- **Clarity:** Design templates that are easy to read and interpret, avoiding overly complex layouts.
- **Visualization:** Incorporate visual elements such as charts, graphs, and tables to enhance understanding.

5. Establishing Review and Approval Protocols

A robust cost reporting framework includes established protocols for the review and approval of cost reports. This ensures that the reports are accurate, comprehensive, and compliant with organizational policies and standards.

Protocol Elements:

- **Review Process:** Define who will review the reports and what criteria will be used.
- **Approval Hierarchy:** Establish an approval hierarchy to ensure accountability.
- **Feedback Mechanism:** Implement a mechanism for reviewers to provide feedback and request clarifications.

6. Training and Capacity Building

Ensuring that all relevant personnel are adequately trained in the cost reporting framework is crucial for its successful implementation. Training should cover the use of reporting tools and software, understanding cost structures, and the process of generating and interpreting reports.

Training Focus Areas:

- **Tool Proficiency:** Training on the specific software and tools used for cost reporting.

- **Framework Understanding:** Education on the overall cost reporting framework, including objectives, processes, and templates.
- **Continuous Learning:** Encourage ongoing training and capacity building to adapt to new tools and processes.

7. Monitoring and Continuous Improvement

Finally, a cost reporting framework should include mechanisms for monitoring its effectiveness and incorporating continuous improvements. Regularly reviewing the framework and soliciting feedback from users helps identify areas for enhancement and ensures that the reporting process evolves with the needs of the project and organization.

Improvement Strategies:

- **Regular Audits:** Conduct regular audits of the cost reporting process to identify and address issues.
- **User Feedback:** Gather feedback from report users to understand their needs and challenges.
- **Benchmarking:** Compare the framework against industry best practices and standards to identify improvement opportunities.

Developing a comprehensive cost reporting framework is critical for effective project cost management. By establishing clear objectives, defining cost structures, implementing reliable data collection processes, designing standardized templates, and incorporating review protocols, organizations can ensure that cost information is accurate, timely, and useful. Training and continuous improvement further enhance the framework's effectiveness, supporting better financial decision-making and project success. As we move forward, understanding the nuances of cost reporting and communication will enable project teams to maintain financial control and transparency, ultimately leading to more successful project outcomes.

Communication Strategies for Cost Management

Effective communication is the cornerstone of successful cost management. It ensures that all stakeholders are informed, engaged, and aligned with the project's financial objectives. This section delves into the communication strategies essential for conveying cost-related information clearly and effectively.

Establishing clear communication channels is vital for facilitating effective cost management. This involves defining the pathways through which information flows between project teams, management, and external stakeholders. Key components of this strategy include designating specific individuals or roles responsible for communicating cost information, utilizing platforms such as email, project management software, and meetings for regular updates, and ensuring that cost information is easily accessible to those who need it without unnecessary barriers.

Different stakeholders have varying levels of interest and expertise in cost management. Therefore, tailoring messages to meet the needs and understanding of each audience is crucial for effective communication. For senior management, providing high-level overviews that highlight key financial metrics and project status is essential. In contrast, project managers and financial analysts benefit from comprehensive reports with detailed breakdowns of costs and variances. For non-technical stakeholders, using simplified language and visuals can effectively convey essential information.

Consistency in communication helps build trust and ensures that stakeholders are always informed about the project's financial status. Establishing a regular reporting schedule is key to maintaining this consistency. Scheduled updates at regular intervals, such as weekly or monthly, help keep everyone on the same page. Regular meetings to discuss cost reports, address concerns, and answer questions further enhance this consistency. Being prepared to provide updates outside of the regular schedule when significant cost changes or issues arise is also important.

Visual aids such as charts, graphs, and dashboards can significantly enhance the clarity and impact of cost reports. Visuals make complex data more accessible and easier to understand. Effective use of visuals includes employing line graphs for trends over time, bar charts for comparing categories, and pie charts for illustrating proportions. Interactive dashboards that allow stakeholders to explore data and drill down into specifics, as well as infographics to summarize key points and highlight critical financial information, are also effective tools.

Transparency in cost management fosters trust and accountability. Clear communication about costs, variances, and financial decisions helps build stakeholder confidence. Transparency tactics include providing stakeholders with access to cost management tools and data as appropriate, maintaining comprehensive documentation of cost assumptions, methodologies, and decisions, and reporting both positive and negative financial information candidly to avoid surprises.

Effective cost management communication is not a one-way street. Encouraging feedback and dialogue ensures that stakeholders can voice concerns, ask questions, and contribute to financial decision-making. Engagement techniques such as implementing mechanisms for stakeholders to provide feedback on cost reports and communication methods, conducting interactive sessions like workshops and Q&A forums to discuss cost management, and promptly addressing queries and concerns raised by stakeholders demonstrate responsiveness and commitment.

Projects and their financial landscapes are dynamic, and communication strategies must adapt accordingly. Regularly reviewing and adjusting communication practices ensures they remain effective and relevant. Adaptation approaches include periodically reviewing communication strategies in project team meetings, using surveys to gather input on the effectiveness of communication practices and identify areas for improvement, and implementing changes based on feedback and evolving project requirements to enhance communication.

Effective communication strategies are integral to successful cost management. Establishing clear channels, tailoring messages to different audiences, leveraging visual aids, ensuring transparency, and encouraging two-way communication help maintain alignment and foster stakeholder trust. Regular reviews and adaptations of communication practices ensure they remain effective in the face of changing project dynamics. Mastering these strategies enables teams to convey critical cost information clearly and efficiently, ultimately contributing to better financial control and project success.

Challenges in Cost Reporting and Communication

Navigating the complexities of cost reporting and communication presents numerous challenges that project managers and financial professionals must address to ensure accurate and effective dissemination of financial information. Understanding and mitigating these challenges are crucial for maintaining the integrity of cost management processes.

One of the primary challenges in cost reporting is the sheer complexity of the data involved. Projects often generate vast amounts of financial data from various sources, including procurement, labour, materials, and overheads. Consolidating this data into coherent and meaningful reports requires sophisticated systems and a high level of expertise. The challenge is compounded when data from disparate systems need to be integrated, necessitating robust data management practices and advanced analytical tools.

Ensuring the accuracy and timeliness of cost reports is another significant challenge. Inaccurate data can lead to misguided decisions, while delays in reporting can prevent timely interventions that could correct course and mitigate issues. This necessitates stringent data validation processes and efficient workflows that facilitate rapid compilation and distribution of reports. Regular audits and real-time data tracking can help in maintaining high standards of accuracy and timeliness.

Engaging stakeholders with cost reports is crucial yet challenging. Different stakeholders, ranging from executives to project managers and external partners, have varying needs and levels of financial literacy. Crafting reports that are detailed enough for in-depth analysis while being accessible and understandable to non-financial stakeholders requires careful consideration and often, iterative feedback loops to refine reporting practices.

Communication gaps can significantly hinder the effectiveness of cost reporting. These gaps may arise from cultural differences, language barriers, or simply misaligned expectations regarding the format and content of reports. Addressing these gaps requires proactive communication strategies, including regular meetings, clear documentation, and possibly, training sessions to ensure all parties are on the same page.

Projects are dynamic by nature, with scopes, schedules, and budgets frequently undergoing changes. Adapting cost reports to reflect these changes in a timely manner is a constant challenge. This requires flexible reporting frameworks that can accommodate changes without compromising on accuracy or completeness. Regular updates and a robust change management process are essential to keep cost reports relevant and up to date.

Integrating various technological tools used for cost management can be challenging. Different tools may have different data formats, user interfaces, and reporting capabilities. Achieving seamless integration to provide a unified view of project costs demands significant effort in terms of system compatibility, data synchronization, and user training. Selecting the right combination of tools and ensuring they work together harmoniously is critical for effective cost reporting.

Maintaining the confidentiality and security of financial data is paramount, especially in industries with stringent regulatory requirements. Ensuring that cost reports are securely transmitted and stored, while still being accessible to authorized personnel, presents a complex challenge. This requires robust cybersecurity measures, secure communication channels, and strict access controls to protect sensitive financial information.

The challenges in cost reporting and communication are multifaceted, involving data complexity, accuracy, stakeholder engagement, communication gaps, changing project dynamics, technological integration, and data security. Addressing these challenges requires a combination of advanced tools, robust processes, and clear communication strategies. By understanding and proactively managing these challenges, project managers and financial professionals can ensure that cost reports are accurate, timely, and effective in supporting decision-making and maintaining financial control.

Continuous Improvement in Cost Reporting

Continuous improvement is essential for enhancing the effectiveness and efficiency of cost reporting processes. By consistently evaluating and refining reporting practices, organizations can ensure that cost reports remain relevant, accurate, and valuable for decision-making. This section explores strategies for driving continuous improvement in cost reporting.

Regular review and evaluation of existing cost reporting processes are fundamental to identifying areas for improvement. This involves analysing the effectiveness of current reporting formats, data collection methods, and dissemination channels. Stakeholder feedback and input are invaluable during this process, providing insights into user needs and preferences.

Benchmarking against industry peers and best practices can offer valuable insights into how other organizations approach cost reporting. Comparing reporting metrics, formats, and processes can highlight areas where improvements can be made. By adopting proven best practices, organizations can streamline their reporting processes and enhance the quality of their cost reports.

The **adoption of advanced technologies** can significantly improve the efficiency and accuracy of cost reporting. Implementing integrated software solutions for data collection, analysis, and visualization can automate manual tasks, reduce errors, and provide real-time insights into project costs. Machine learning and artificial intelligence can further enhance predictive analytics capabilities, enabling organizations to anticipate cost trends and potential deviations.

Investing in **training and skill development** for employees involved in cost reporting is essential for driving continuous improvement. Providing training on new reporting tools and techniques, as well as financial analysis methodologies, can empower staff to generate more insightful and actionable cost reports. Cross-functional training initiatives can also foster collaboration and knowledge sharing across different departments.

Process optimization involves streamlining and standardizing cost reporting workflows to eliminate inefficiencies and redundancies. This may involve reengineering reporting processes, clarifying roles and responsibilities, and establishing clear guidelines for data collection and validation. Automation of routine tasks and the introduction of workflow management tools can further enhance process efficiency.

Establishing **feedback mechanisms** for stakeholders to provide input on cost reports is critical for driving continuous improvement. Soliciting feedback through surveys, focus groups, or regular meetings allows organizations to identify areas for improvement and address user needs and preferences. Incorporating feedback loops into reporting processes ensures that cost reports remain relevant and useful over time.

Continuous monitoring of cost reporting performance metrics is essential for assessing the effectiveness of reporting practices. Key performance indicators such as report accuracy, timeliness, and user satisfaction can provide insights into areas requiring improvement. By tracking these metrics over time, organizations can identify trends and patterns, enabling them to make data-driven decisions to optimize their reporting processes.

In today's dynamic business environment, organizations must be **agile and adaptive** in their approach to cost reporting. This involves embracing change and responding quickly to evolving stakeholder needs and market dynamics. Adopting agile methodologies for reporting process development and enhancement can facilitate rapid iteration and improvement, ensuring that cost reports remain relevant and impactful.

Continuous improvement is essential for enhancing the effectiveness and efficiency of cost reporting processes. By regularly reviewing and evaluating existing practices, benchmarking against industry best practices, leveraging technology, investing in training and skill development, optimizing processes, soliciting stakeholder feedback, monitoring performance metrics, and embracing agile adaptation, organizations can drive ongoing improvement in their cost reporting capabilities. By continuously striving for excellence in cost reporting, organizations can ensure that their cost reports remain valuable tools for decision-making and financial control.

In conclusion, effective cost reporting and communication are essential components of successful project management and financial control. Throughout this chapter, we have explored various strategies and challenges related to cost reporting and communication, highlighting the importance of clear, timely, and accurate financial information.

Cost reporting serves as a critical tool for monitoring project finances, identifying cost trends, and facilitating decision-making. By providing stakeholders with insights into project costs, variances, and financial performance, cost reports enable informed decision-making and proactive management of project budgets.

Communication plays a pivotal role in ensuring that cost reports are understood and acted upon by relevant stakeholders. Tailoring messages to different audiences, leveraging visual aids, and establishing clear communication channels are essential for effective communication of cost-related information.

However, the journey towards effective cost reporting and communication is not without its challenges. Complexity of data, accuracy and timeliness, stakeholder engagement, communication gaps, changing project dynamics, technological integration, confidentiality, and security are among the key challenges that organizations must address.

To overcome these challenges and drive continuous improvement, organizations must embrace a holistic approach to cost reporting and communication. This includes regular review and evaluation of existing processes, benchmarking against industry best practices, adoption of advanced technologies, investment in training and skill development, process optimization, solicitation of stakeholder feedback, monitoring of performance metrics, and agile adaptation to changing circumstances.

By implementing these strategies and addressing the challenges proactively, organizations can enhance the effectiveness and efficiency of their cost reporting and communication practices. Ultimately, this enables better financial control, informed decision-making, and successful project outcomes.

In summary, effective cost reporting and communication are foundational pillars of sound project management and financial governance. By prioritizing these aspects and continuously striving for improvement, organizations can maximize their chances of project success and achieve their strategic objectives.

CHAPTER 8: SUSTAINABILITY AND COST MANAGEMENT

Introduction to Sustainability and Cost Management

Sustainability has become a cornerstone of modern project management, driving the evolution of how costs are planned, managed, and controlled. In the context of cost management, sustainability refers to practices that not only meet the economic goals of a project but also address environmental and social impacts. Integrating sustainability into cost management ensures that projects are not only economically viable but also environmentally responsible and socially beneficial.

The importance of embedding sustainability into cost management cannot be overstated. It allows organizations to achieve long-term savings, enhance their reputation, and comply with increasing regulatory demands. Sustainable cost management practices can lead to significant reductions in energy use, waste, and resource consumption, thereby lowering operational costs over the project lifecycle.

Aligning cost management with sustainability objectives involves a comprehensive approach. This includes assessing the environmental impact of materials and processes, considering social implications such as community well-being and labour practices, and incorporating these factors into the project budget and financial planning. By doing so, organizations can ensure that their projects contribute positively to the environment and society while remaining within budget and achieving business goals.

Moreover, sustainability in cost management is not just about compliance or corporate social responsibility; it is about future-proofing projects against risks associated with resource scarcity, climate change, and evolving regulations. As businesses and stakeholders increasingly prioritize sustainability, integrating these principles into cost management becomes essential for competitive advantage and long-term success.

In this chapter, we will explore the various dimensions of sustainability in cost management, examine the cost implications of sustainable practices, and provide strategies for integrating environmental and social costs into project budgeting. We will also discuss how sustainable design and construction can lead to cost savings, and present tools and technologies that support sustainable cost management. Through case studies and practical examples, we will illustrate the challenges and best practices in achieving sustainable cost management.

Cost Implications of Sustainable Practices

The adoption of sustainable practices in project management has a profound impact on costs. While there is often a perception that sustainability increases expenses, a closer analysis reveals a more nuanced picture where long-term savings can outweigh initial investments.

Short-Term Costs vs. Long-Term Savings

Implementing sustainable practices typically involves higher upfront costs. These can include expenses for eco-friendly materials, energy-efficient technologies, and sustainable design features. For example, green building materials may cost more than conventional options, and installing renewable energy systems like solar panels requires significant investment.

However, these initial costs are often offset by long-term savings. Energy-efficient buildings, for instance, incur lower utility bills due to reduced energy consumption. Over time, the savings on operating costs can surpass the initial expenditures. Additionally, sustainable practices often lead to lower maintenance costs and longer lifespans for building components, contributing to further savings.

Economic Benefits of Sustainability

Sustainable practices can also offer substantial economic benefits beyond direct cost savings. Projects that prioritize sustainability often attract incentives such as tax breaks, grants, and subsidies from governments and other organizations. These financial incentives can significantly reduce the net costs of implementing sustainable measures.

Furthermore, projects that achieve certifications like BREEAM (Building Research Establishment Environmental Assessment Method) can enhance an organization's reputation. This improved image can lead to increased marketability and higher property values, providing additional economic advantages.

Examples of Sustainable Practices

1. **Energy Efficiency:** Incorporating energy-efficient systems, such as LED lighting, advanced HVAC systems, and smart building technologies, reduces energy consumption and costs. These systems not only lower energy bills but also reduce greenhouse gas emissions, contributing to environmental sustainability.

2. **Water Conservation:** Implementing water-saving fixtures and systems, such as low-flow toilets and rainwater harvesting, reduces water usage and utility costs. Sustainable landscaping practices that require less irrigation further contribute to water conservation and cost savings.

3. **Waste Reduction:** Sustainable waste management practices, including recycling and composting, minimize the

volume of waste sent to landfills. This can reduce disposal costs and create opportunities for revenue through the sale of recyclable materials.

4. **Sustainable Sourcing:** Choosing materials and products with lower environmental impacts, such as recycled content or sustainably harvested wood, can reduce the ecological footprint of a project. Sustainable sourcing can also enhance supply chain resilience and reduce the risk of supply disruptions.

The cost implications of sustainable practices extend beyond the immediate financial outlay. By considering the full lifecycle of a project, including operational and maintenance costs, it becomes clear that sustainability can lead to significant economic benefits. Sustainable practices not only contribute to environmental and social well-being but also enhance the financial performance of projects, making them a smart investment for the future.

Integrating Environmental and Social Costs into Project Budgeting

Integrating environmental and social costs into project budgeting is essential for achieving sustainability in cost management. This process involves evaluating and accounting for the broader impacts of a project beyond the immediate financial costs, ensuring that projects contribute positively to the environment and society while remaining economically viable.

Environmental costs refer to the negative impacts of a project on natural resources and ecosystems. These can include emissions of greenhouse gases, pollution, resource depletion, and habitat destruction. Social costs encompass the effects on communities and individuals, such as health impacts, displacement, job creation, and social equity.

Incorporating these costs into project budgeting requires a comprehensive understanding of their implications and the methodologies to quantify them. This ensures that the true cost of a project is reflected, accounting for its long-term impacts on the environment and society.

The first step is to identify the specific environmental and social costs associated with the project. This involves considering factors such as emissions, waste generation, water usage, and community displacement. Engaging with stakeholders, including environmental experts and community representatives, can provide valuable insights into these costs.

Once identified, the next step is to quantify these costs. Converting qualitative impacts into monetary values can be challenging, but techniques such as lifecycle assessment (LCA) for environmental impacts and social return on investment (SROI) for social impacts can be used to estimate these costs. Quantification ensures that these impacts are not merely acknowledged but are integrated into the financial planning and decision-making processes.

After quantification, these costs should be integrated into the project budget. This can be done by adding line items for environmental and social costs or by adjusting the overall budget to reflect these considerations. It is crucial to ensure that these costs are not treated as externalities but are included in the financial planning and decision-making processes. Using environmental and social accounting frameworks, such as Triple Bottom Line (TBL) accounting, can help integrate these costs systematically. TBL accounting considers economic, environmental, and social dimensions, providing a more holistic view of project performance.

Various tools and methodologies can assist in integrating environmental and social costs into project budgeting. Lifecycle Assessment (LCA) evaluates the environmental impacts of a product or project throughout its lifecycle, from raw material extraction to disposal. It helps quantify emissions, energy use, and other environmental impacts, providing a comprehensive view of the environmental costs. Social Return on Investment

(SROI) measures the social value created by a project, converting social outcomes into monetary terms. It helps quantify the social impacts, such as job creation, health improvements, and community benefits, and integrates these into the financial analysis. Environmental Impact Assessment (EIA) evaluates the potential environmental impacts of a project before its implementation. It identifies significant environmental risks and provides recommendations for mitigation, helping to integrate these considerations into project planning and budgeting.

Expanding on these methodologies, LCA provides a detailed analysis of environmental impacts across the entire lifecycle of a project, from raw material extraction to disposal. This comprehensive approach ensures that all environmental costs are accounted for, helping to identify opportunities for reducing negative impacts. SROI offers a framework for quantifying the social benefits of a project, such as improved community health, increased employment opportunities, and enhanced social equity. By converting these social outcomes into monetary terms, SROI enables project managers to incorporate these benefits into their budgeting and decision-making processes. EIA, on the other hand, focuses on identifying and mitigating potential environmental risks before a project is implemented. By conducting thorough assessments and recommending mitigation measures, EIA helps ensure that environmental considerations are integrated into project planning and budgeting from the outset.

Integrating environmental and social costs into project budgeting is crucial for achieving sustainable cost management. By identifying, quantifying, and incorporating these costs, projects can ensure that they are not only economically viable but also environmentally responsible and socially beneficial. This approach helps create a more accurate and comprehensive view of project costs, leading to better decision-making and more sustainable outcomes.

Achieving Cost Savings through Sustainable Design and Construction

Sustainable design and construction benefit the environment and society while leading to significant cost savings over the lifecycle of a project. By incorporating sustainability principles into design and construction practices, projects can reduce resource consumption, lower operational costs, and enhance long-term value.

Sustainable design focuses on creating buildings and infrastructure that minimize environmental impact and promote resource efficiency. Key principles include energy efficiency, water conservation, the use of sustainable materials, and enhancing indoor environmental quality. These principles can be integrated into every phase of a project, from planning and design to construction and operation.

One of the most effective ways to achieve cost savings is through **energy-efficient design**. This includes using high-performance building envelopes, energy-efficient HVAC systems, and renewable energy sources like solar or wind power. Implementing these measures can significantly reduce energy consumption and lower utility bills over the building's lifecycle. For example, incorporating passive solar design strategies, such as optimizing building orientation and incorporating shading devices, can reduce the need for artificial heating and cooling, leading to substantial energy savings. Additionally, energy-efficient lighting solutions, such as LED lighting and smart lighting controls, further contribute to reducing energy usage and operational costs.

Water-efficient design and construction practices also contribute to cost savings. Strategies include installing low-flow fixtures, using native landscaping that requires less irrigation, and implementing rainwater harvesting systems. These measures reduce water consumption and lower water bills while also reducing the strain on local water resources.

Additionally, the use of greywater recycling systems can further enhance water efficiency by reusing wastewater for non-potable purposes, such as irrigation and toilet flushing. Advanced irrigation technologies, such as drip irrigation and soil moisture sensors, can also optimize water use and prevent overwatering, further conserving water resources and reducing costs.

Using **sustainable and locally sourced materials** can reduce transportation costs and environmental impact. Materials such as recycled steel, reclaimed wood, and low-VOC (volatile organic compound) paints contribute to a healthier indoor environment and reduce waste. Additionally, selecting durable materials that require less maintenance and have a longer lifespan can lower replacement costs and reduce the overall lifecycle cost of a building. The integration of materials with high thermal mass, such as concrete and brick, can improve a building's energy efficiency by regulating indoor temperatures and reducing the need for heating and cooling.

Designing for improved **indoor environmental quality (IEQ)** can lead to cost savings through increased occupant productivity and reduced healthcare costs. Strategies include maximizing natural light, improving ventilation, and using non-toxic materials. Healthier indoor environments can reduce absenteeism and improve overall well-being, which translates into economic benefits for building owners and tenants. Implementing biophilic design elements, such as incorporating plants and natural materials, can also enhance the aesthetic and psychological benefits, contributing to a more pleasant and productive indoor environment.

Adopting **innovative construction practices**, such as prefabrication and modular construction, can also lead to cost savings. These methods reduce construction time, minimize waste, and improve quality control. For instance, prefabrication allows for the production of building components in a controlled environment, reducing weather-related delays and material waste. Additionally, modular construction enables faster assembly on-site, reducing labour costs and accelerating project timelines. Advanced construction technologies, such as 3D printing and robotic automation, can further enhance efficiency and precision, leading to additional cost savings and reduced material waste.

A comprehensive approach to achieving cost savings through sustainable design and construction involves conducting a **lifecycle cost analysis (LCCA)**. LCCA evaluates the total cost of ownership over the life of a project, including initial construction costs, operating costs, maintenance, and end-of-life disposal. By considering the long-term financial benefits of sustainable features, project managers can make informed decisions that optimize both environmental and economic performance. This analysis can also identify potential trade-offs and synergies between different sustainability measures, ensuring a balanced and cost-effective approach to sustainable design.

Sustainable design and construction practices extend beyond initial cost savings to **operational efficiency and maintenance**. Buildings designed with sustainability in mind often require less frequent maintenance and have lower operating costs due to the use of durable materials and efficient systems. For example, energy-efficient HVAC systems not only reduce energy consumption but also require less maintenance compared to conventional systems. Sustainable landscaping practices, such as xeriscaping and the use of drought-resistant plants, can reduce the need for irrigation and maintenance, further lowering operational costs.

Achieving cost savings through sustainable design and construction also involves **engaging stakeholders and raising awareness** about the benefits of sustainability. Educating clients, tenants, and facility managers about sustainable practices can encourage the adoption of energy-saving behaviours and proper maintenance practices, leading to additional cost savings. Stakeholder engagement can also facilitate the acceptance and support of sustainability initiatives, ensuring their successful implementation and long-term benefits.

Achieving cost savings through sustainable design and construction requires a holistic approach that integrates energy efficiency, water conservation, sustainable materials, and innovative construction practices. By adopting these principles, projects can reduce resource consumption, lower operational costs, and enhance long-term value. Sustainable design and construction not only benefit the environment and society but also offer significant economic advantages, making them a smart investment for the future. Implementing these strategies in a comprehensive and well-coordinated manner ensures that projects can achieve both financial and environmental sustainability, ultimately leading to a more sustainable and cost-effective built environment.

Life Cycle Cost Analysis (LCCA)

Life Cycle Cost Analysis (LCCA) serves as a cornerstone in sustainable cost management, offering a comprehensive evaluation of a project's total cost over its entire lifespan. LCCA allows project managers to make informed decisions by considering all expenses from inception to disposal, providing a nuanced financial perspective.

The Importance of LCCA in Sustainable Projects: LCCA holds particular significance in sustainable projects where upfront investments in environmentally friendly practices may obscure long-term savings. For instance, while incorporating energy-efficient systems may entail higher initial costs, the subsequent reduction in utility expenses can yield substantial net savings. LCCA captures these long-term benefits, offering a holistic view of a project's financial viability.

Key Components of LCCA: LCCA encompasses several essential components:

- **Initial Costs:** Covering planning, design, and

construction expenses.

- **Operational Costs:** Including utilities, maintenance, and repairs.
- **Replacement and End-of-Life Costs:** Accounting for future component replacements and disposal expenses.
- **Residual Value:** Assessing the value of the building or its components at the end of their lifespan.

Conducting LCCA: Conducting LCCA involves defining the project scope, identifying all relevant costs, determining an appropriate discount rate, calculating present values, performing sensitivity analysis, and interpreting results. This comprehensive process enables project teams to evaluate cost-saving opportunities and make informed decisions.

Benefits of LCCA: LCCA promotes transparency and accountability by outlining the financial implications of different design choices. It encourages the adoption of energy-efficient systems, durable materials, and innovative construction methods, ultimately leading to lower lifecycle costs and enhanced project value.

Challenges and Best Practices: Implementing LCCA poses challenges due to the complexity of accurately estimating long-term costs and benefits. To address these challenges, best practices include using reliable data, engaging experts, and regularly updating the analysis to reflect changing project conditions.

Incorporating Life Cycle Cost Analysis into project planning fosters sustainable practices and drives cost-effective decision-making. As the construction industry prioritizes sustainability, LCCA will continue to play a vital role in delivering environmentally responsible projects with long-term financial benefits.

Sustainable Procurement Practices

Sustainable procurement is not just a trend; it's a strategic approach that organizations adopt to ensure that their purchasing decisions align with environmental, social, and economic considerations. It involves integrating sustainability principles into the procurement process, from selecting suppliers to managing contracts and supplier relationships. By prioritizing sustainability, organizations can minimize negative impacts on the environment, support local communities, and drive long-term cost savings.

Understanding Sustainable Procurement:

Sustainable procurement goes beyond traditional cost considerations; it encompasses a broader set of criteria that evaluate suppliers' environmental, social, and ethical practices. This approach seeks to balance economic objectives with environmental and social responsibilities, recognizing that sustainable supply chains are essential for long-term business success. Sustainable procurement practices extend across various industries, from construction and manufacturing to hospitality and healthcare.

Key Principles of Sustainable Procurement:

1. Environmental Responsibility: Sustainable procurement involves selecting products and services that have minimal environmental impact throughout their lifecycle. This includes assessing factors such as resource consumption, energy efficiency, waste generation, and emissions.

2. Social Equity: Organizations must consider the social implications of their procurement decisions, including labour practices, human rights, and community engagement. Ethical sourcing practices prioritize fair labour conditions, diversity and inclusion, and support for local communities.

3. Economic Viability: While sustainability is a priority, procurement decisions must also be economically viable. Sustainable procurement aims to achieve value for money by balancing upfront costs with long-term benefits, such as reduced operating expenses and enhanced brand reputation.

Practices for Integrating Sustainability into Procurement:

1. **Supplier Evaluation and Selection:** Develop robust criteria for evaluating suppliers based on their sustainability performance. Consider factors such as environmental certifications, adherence to labour standards, ethical sourcing practices, and commitment to sustainability goals.

2. **Lifecycle Analysis:** Conduct lifecycle assessments to evaluate the environmental impacts of products and services over their entire lifecycle. This analysis considers the extraction of raw materials, manufacturing processes, transportation, product use, and end-of-life disposal.

3. **Green Procurement Policies:** Implement policies and guidelines that prioritize the purchase of sustainable products and services. This may involve setting targets for reducing waste, increasing energy efficiency, and promoting the use of renewable resources.

4. **Supplier Engagement and Collaboration:** Collaborate with suppliers to promote sustainability throughout the supply chain. Encourage suppliers to adopt environmentally friendly practices, improve transparency, and share best practices.

5. **Transparency and Reporting:** Enhance transparency in procurement processes by disclosing information about supplier selection criteria, sustainability performance, and supply chain practices. Regular reporting on sustainability initiatives and progress toward goals builds trust with stakeholders.

Benefits of Sustainable Procurement:

- **Cost Savings:** Sustainable procurement practices can lead to cost savings through reduced energy consumption, waste reduction, and operational efficiency improvements.

- **Risk Mitigation:** By diversifying supply chains and selecting suppliers with robust sustainability practices, organizations can mitigate risks related to regulatory compliance, reputational damage, and supply chain disruptions.

- **Brand Reputation:** Embracing sustainable procurement enhances brand reputation and credibility, attracting environmentally conscious customers and investors.
- **Compliance and Stakeholder Expectations:** Sustainable procurement practices help organizations comply with environmental regulations and meet stakeholder expectations for corporate social responsibility.

Sustainable procurement is a strategic imperative for organizations seeking to align their purchasing decisions with environmental, social, and economic objectives. By integrating sustainability into procurement processes, organizations can drive positive environmental and social impacts while achieving long-term cost savings and enhancing their reputation. Embracing sustainable procurement practices is not only essential for business success but also contributes to a more sustainable and equitable future for all.

Regulatory and Compliance Considerations

In the realm of sustainability and cost management, navigating regulatory frameworks and compliance requirements is paramount. Understanding and adhering to regulations not only ensures legal compliance but also demonstrates a commitment to responsible business practices and sustainability goals.

Sustainability initiatives intersect with a myriad of regulations at local, national, and international levels. These regulations span environmental protection, employment practices, health and safety standards, and ethical sourcing. Organizations must stay abreast of evolving regulatory landscapes to ensure compliance and avoid potential penalties or reputational damage.

Environmental regulations encompass a wide range of laws aimed at protecting natural resources, reducing pollution, and mitigating climate change. These regulations may include emission standards, waste management protocols, energy efficiency requirements, and restrictions on hazardous substances. Compliance with environmental regulations often requires implementing sustainable practices, such as reducing carbon emissions, conserving water resources, and minimizing waste generation.

Employment regulations focus on ensuring fair and safe working conditions for employees throughout the supply chain. These standards encompass aspects such as minimum wage requirements, working hours, occupational health and safety, and child labour laws. Additionally, organizations must uphold human rights principles, including non-discrimination and freedom of association.

In an era of increasing scrutiny, **ethical sourcing** practices are gaining prominence. Regulatory frameworks promote transparency and accountability in supply chains by requiring organizations to disclose information about suppliers' employment practices, environmental impacts, and social responsibility efforts. Compliance with these regulations entails implementing robust supplier verification processes, conducting due diligence assessments, and engaging in dialogue with stakeholders.

With the proliferation of digital technologies, **data privacy and security regulations** are becoming increasingly stringent. Organizations must safeguard sensitive information, including customer data, employee records, and intellectual property, from unauthorized access or misuse. Compliance with data protection regulations, such as the General Data Protection Regulation (GDPR) in the European Union or the California Consumer Privacy Act (CCPA) in the United States, requires implementing robust data management practices and ensuring transparency in data collection and processing activities.

Operating in a global marketplace necessitates compliance with diverse regulatory frameworks across different jurisdictions. Organizations with international supply chains must navigate a complex web of regulations, trade agreements, and cultural norms. Compliance with global standards, such as the United Nations Global Compact or the International Labour Organization's conventions, requires a deep understanding of local laws and customs, as well as a commitment to upholding universal human rights and sustainable development goals.

Navigating regulatory and compliance considerations in sustainability and cost management requires a proactive approach and a commitment to upholding ethical standards and legal requirements. By staying informed about evolving regulations, implementing robust compliance programs, and fostering transparency and accountability throughout the supply chain, organizations can mitigate risks, build trust with stakeholders, and drive sustainable business practices forward.

Tools and Technologies for Sustainable Cost Management

In today's rapidly evolving business landscape, organizations are increasingly leveraging tools and technologies to integrate sustainability considerations into their cost management practices. These tools enable organizations to track environmental and social impacts, optimize resource utilization, and make data-driven decisions to achieve sustainable outcomes while managing costs effectively.

Lifecycle assessment software enables organizations to evaluate the environmental impacts of products, services, and processes throughout their lifecycle. By analysing factors such as raw material extraction, production, distribution, use, and disposal, LCA software helps identify opportunities for reducing environmental footprints and optimizing resource efficiency. These insights inform decision-making processes and support the development of sustainable products and practices.

Carbon accounting and management tools allow organizations to measure, monitor, and manage their carbon emissions and carbon footprint. These tools track greenhouse gas emissions across the value chain, identify emission hotspots, and quantify the environmental impact of business activities. By implementing carbon accounting software, organizations can set emission reduction targets, track progress towards sustainability goals, and identify opportunities for carbon footprint reduction and offsetting.

Sustainability reporting platforms facilitate the collection, analysis, and reporting of environmental, social, and governance (ESG) data. These platforms enable organizations to generate comprehensive sustainability reports that communicate their performance, initiatives, and impacts to stakeholders, including investors, customers, and regulators. By centralizing sustainability data and streamlining reporting processes, these platforms enhance transparency, accountability, and credibility in sustainability disclosures.

Supply chain management systems integrate sustainability considerations into procurement, sourcing, and supplier management processes. These systems enable organizations to assess supplier performance based on environmental, social, and ethical criteria, such as carbon emissions, employment practices, and product certifications. By optimizing supply chain transparency and visibility, organizations can identify risks, improve supplier relationships, and drive sustainability across the value chain.

Renewable energy and energy management software help organizations optimize energy consumption, reduce energy costs, and transition to renewable energy sources. These tools enable organizations to monitor energy usage, identify energy-saving opportunities, and implement energy efficiency measures. By analysing energy data and implementing renewable energy projects, organizations can reduce their environmental impact, lower operational costs, and enhance their resilience to energy price fluctuations.

Integrated sustainability platforms provide comprehensive solutions for managing sustainability initiatives, metrics, and performance indicators. These platforms offer functionalities such as sustainability goal setting, performance tracking, stakeholder engagement, and scenario analysis. By centralizing sustainability data and analytics, organizations can drive continuous improvement, align sustainability efforts with business objectives, and demonstrate leadership in sustainable practices.

Tools and technologies play a pivotal role in enabling organizations to integrate sustainability considerations into cost management practices effectively. By leveraging advanced software solutions, organizations can track environmental and social impacts, optimize resource utilization, and make informed decisions that drive sustainable outcomes while managing costs efficiently. As sustainability becomes increasingly integral to business success, investing in tools and technologies for sustainable cost management is essential for organizations seeking to thrive in a rapidly changing global landscape.

Challenges and Best Practices

Navigating the intersection of sustainability and cost management presents organizations with a myriad of challenges and opportunities. Understanding these challenges and adopting best practices is crucial for effectively integrating sustainability into cost management strategies and driving meaningful impact.

Challenges:

1. **Cost-Effectiveness:** Balancing sustainability objectives with cost considerations can be challenging, especially when sustainable alternatives entail higher upfront costs. Organizations must carefully evaluate the long-term benefits and trade-offs associated with sustainability initiatives to ensure cost-effectiveness.

2.   **Data Availability and Quality:** Obtaining accurate and reliable data on environmental and social impacts can be challenging, particularly in complex supply chains. Limited data availability and inconsistencies in reporting standards pose barriers to effective sustainability measurement and reporting.

3.   **Regulatory Complexity:** Navigating a complex regulatory landscape, characterized by evolving environmental, social, and governance (ESG) requirements, presents compliance challenges for organizations. Adhering to diverse regulations across jurisdictions requires a deep understanding of legal requirements and proactive risk management strategies.

4.   **Supply Chain Transparency:** Achieving transparency and visibility across global supply chains is a significant challenge for organizations seeking to integrate sustainability into cost management. Limited visibility into supplier practices and dependencies can hinder efforts to identify risks, assess impacts, and drive sustainable procurement practices.

5.   **Behavioural Change:** Effecting behavioural change within organizations and among stakeholders is essential for driving sustainability initiatives forward. Overcoming resistance to change, fostering a culture of sustainability, and engaging stakeholders effectively require strong leadership, communication, and collaboration.

Best Practices:

1.   **Leadership Commitment:** Demonstrating leadership commitment to sustainability is essential for driving organizational change and fostering a culture of sustainability. Executive buy-in, clear sustainability goals, and dedicated resources signal organizational priorities and set the tone for sustainability initiatives.

2.   **Integrated Approach:** Adopting an integrated approach to sustainability and cost management ensures that sustainability considerations are embedded across business functions and processes. Integrating sustainability into

strategic planning, decision-making, and performance management fosters alignment with business objectives and enhances overall effectiveness.

3. **Stakeholder Engagement:** Engaging stakeholders, including employees, customers, suppliers, investors, and communities, is critical for driving sustainability initiatives forward. Building partnerships, soliciting feedback, and involving stakeholders in decision-making processes enhance transparency, trust, and accountability.

4. **Continuous Improvement:** Embracing a mindset of continuous improvement enables organizations to adapt to evolving sustainability challenges and seize opportunities for innovation. Implementing robust monitoring, evaluation, and feedback mechanisms facilitates learning, adaptation, and refinement of sustainability strategies over time.

5. **Collaboration and Partnerships:** Collaboration and partnerships with industry peers, governments, non-governmental organizations (NGOs), and academia can amplify the impact of sustainability initiatives. Collaborative initiatives enable knowledge sharing, resource pooling, and collective action to address shared sustainability challenges.

Navigating the challenges and leveraging best practices in sustainability and cost management is essential for organizations seeking to drive sustainable business practices and achieve long-term success. By addressing challenges such as cost-effectiveness, data availability, regulatory complexity, supply chain transparency, and behavioural change, and adopting best practices such as leadership commitment, integrated approach, stakeholder engagement, continuous improvement, and collaboration, organizations can unlock opportunities for sustainable growth and create value for all stakeholders.

In conclusion, sustainability and cost management are

intricately linked concepts that play a pivotal role in shaping the future of business. As organizations navigate an increasingly complex and interconnected global landscape, integrating sustainability considerations into cost management practices is imperative for long-term success and resilience.

Throughout this chapter, we have explored the importance of sustainability in cost management, examining the cost implications of sustainable practices, strategies for integrating environmental and social costs into project budgeting, and approaches for achieving cost savings through sustainable design and construction. We have delved into the role of lifecycle cost analysis, sustainable procurement practices, and regulatory compliance in driving sustainable cost management.

Despite the challenges posed by cost-effectiveness, data availability, regulatory complexity, supply chain transparency, and behavioural change, organizations have the opportunity to leverage best practices such as leadership commitment, integrated approach, stakeholder engagement, continuous improvement, and collaboration to overcome these challenges and drive sustainable outcomes.

As organizations strive to navigate the sustainability landscape and seize opportunities for innovation and growth, it is essential to adopt a holistic approach that considers the interconnectedness of economic, environmental, and social factors. By embracing sustainability as a core business value and integrating it into decision-making processes, organizations can enhance their competitiveness, mitigate risks, and create value for stakeholders across the value chain.

In the journey towards mastering cost management and sustainability, organizations must remain agile, adaptive, and forward-thinking, continuously striving to balance economic prosperity with environmental stewardship and social responsibility. By embracing sustainability as a driver of innovation, efficiency, and resilience, organizations can chart a course towards a more sustainable and prosperous future for themselves and generations to come.

CHAPTER 9: CONTINUOUS IMPROVEMENT IN COST MANAGEMENT

Introduction to Continuous Improvement

Continuous improvement is the cornerstone of effective cost management, enabling organizations to enhance efficiency, optimize resources, and drive sustainable growth. In this section, we delve into the significance of continuous improvement methodologies and their application within cost management practices.

Continuous improvement involves the ongoing evaluation and refinement of processes, practices, and systems to achieve incremental enhancements in performance and outcomes. Within the realm of cost management, this iterative approach plays a crucial role in identifying inefficiencies, reducing waste, and maximizing value delivery.

Continuous improvement methodologies, such as Lean and Six Sigma, offer structured frameworks for driving improvement initiatives. These methodologies are grounded in principles of efficiency, effectiveness, and customer-centricity, providing organizations with systematic approaches to problem-solving and process optimization.

Effective cost management is not solely about minimizing expenses but rather aligning costs with strategic objectives and business priorities. Continuous improvement methodologies facilitate this alignment by fostering a culture of innovation, adaptability, and accountability, ensuring that cost management efforts are tightly integrated with overarching project goals and organizational strategies.

As we delve deeper into the realm of continuous improvement in subsequent sections, we will explore how organizations can leverage these principles and methodologies to enhance cost management practices, drive performance improvements, and achieve sustainable success.

Learning from Cost Overruns and Failures

Cost overruns and project failures are detrimental to organizations, not only in terms of financial losses but also in terms of delays, diminished stakeholder confidence, and reputational damage. These setbacks often stem from various underlying issues within cost management practices.

Diving deep into the root causes of cost overruns and project failures unveils a multitude of factors. Inadequate planning, incomplete scoping, inaccurate estimations, insufficient risk management, and ineffective communication are among the common culprits. Organizations need to conduct meticulous post-mortem analyses to unearth these systemic issues and prevent their recurrence.

Once the causes are identified, organizations can implement targeted strategies for remediation. Strengthening project planning and scoping processes, enhancing risk identification and mitigation strategies, improving communication channels, and bolstering project governance and controls are pivotal. Additionally, fostering a culture of transparency, accountability, and continuous improvement is crucial for addressing these challenges systematically.

Learning from cost overruns and failures should be ingrained in the organization's culture. It entails fostering an environment where mistakes are viewed as opportunities for growth and improvement. Implementing mechanisms like post-project reviews, lessons learned sessions, and knowledge sharing platforms enables organizations to harness valuable insights and translate them into actionable improvements. By nurturing a culture of continuous learning and improvement, organizations can mitigate the recurrence of cost overruns and project failures, thus fostering long-term success and sustainability.

Implementing Lessons Learned for Future Projects

Implementing lessons learned from past projects is pivotal for driving continuous improvement in cost management practices. This section delves into the strategies and methodologies organizations can adopt to translate insights gained from previous experiences into tangible improvements for future projects.

- **Establishing a Framework for Knowledge Capture**

Central to implementing lessons learned is the establishment of a robust framework for knowledge capture and dissemination. Organizations should systematically document insights, best practices, and areas for improvement throughout the project lifecycle. This includes maintaining comprehensive project records, conducting post-mortem reviews, and facilitating knowledge-sharing sessions among project teams.

- **Integration into Project Management Processes**

Lessons learned should not exist in isolation but should be seamlessly integrated into project management processes. Organizations should develop mechanisms to incorporate insights from past projects into future planning, scoping, estimation, and risk management activities. This may involve updating project templates, revising standard operating procedures, and leveraging project management software to facilitate knowledge transfer.

- **Role of Project Retrospectives**

Project retrospectives play a crucial role in facilitating reflection and continuous improvement. These structured sessions provide teams with the opportunity to reflect on project successes, challenges, and lessons learned. By conducting retrospectives at key project milestones, organizations can identify patterns, trends, and areas for improvement, thus enhancing their ability to deliver projects on time and within budget.

- **Cultivating a Learning Culture**

Creating a culture that values and promotes learning is essential for the effective implementation of lessons learned. Organizations should foster an environment where team members feel encouraged to share insights, ask questions, and challenge existing norms. Leaders play a pivotal role in modelling behaviours that promote continuous improvement, such as embracing feedback, embracing experimentation, and recognizing and rewarding learning initiatives.

- **Iterative Improvement and Adaptation**

Continuous improvement is an iterative process that requires ongoing evaluation and adaptation. Organizations should continuously monitor the effectiveness of implemented lessons learned and be prepared to adjust their approaches as needed. This may involve soliciting feedback from project teams, stakeholders, and external experts, and iterating on processes and practices based on observed outcomes.

- **Institutionalizing Change**

To ensure sustainability, organizations must institutionalize changes resulting from lessons learned. This may involve updating organizational policies, procedures, and training programs to reflect new insights and best practices. By embedding continuous improvement principles into the fabric of the organization, companies can foster a culture of innovation, resilience, and adaptability that enables them to thrive in an ever-changing environment.

Professional Development and Certification in Cost Management

Professional development and certification programs play a crucial role in equipping individuals with the knowledge, skills, and credentials necessary to excel in cost management roles. This section explores the significance of continuous learning and certification in fostering expertise and driving excellence in cost management practices.

In today's dynamic business environment, staying abreast of the latest trends, techniques, and technologies is essential for success in cost management. Continuous learning enables professionals to expand their knowledge base, refine their skill set, and adapt to evolving industry standards and best practices. Whether through formal education, workshops, seminars, or self-directed learning initiatives, ongoing professional development is integral to staying competitive and advancing in the field.

Certification programs provide professionals with a structured pathway to demonstrate their proficiency and expertise in cost management. Accredited certifications, such as those offered by professional organizations like the Royal Institute of Chartered Surveyors (RICS), Project Management Institute (PMI), the Association for Advancement of Cost Engineering (AACE International), and the Chartered Institute of Building (CIOB), validate individuals' competency in key areas of cost estimation, budgeting, control, and analysis. By earning recognized certifications, professionals not only enhance their credibility but also gain access to a global network of peers and resources.

Certification offers numerous benefits to both individuals and organizations. For professionals, certification serves as a mark of distinction, signalling their commitment to excellence and adherence to industry standards. It enhances career prospects, increases earning potential, and opens doors to new opportunities. From an organizational perspective, having certified professionals on staff instils confidence in clients and stakeholders, enhances project outcomes, and fosters a culture of professionalism and continuous improvement.

Maintaining certification typically requires professionals to fulfil continuing education requirements, ensuring that they remain current with industry developments and best practices. This may involve completing a certain number of continuing Professional Development (CPDs), attending relevant workshops or conferences, or participating in ongoing professional development activities. By embracing lifelong learning, certified professionals demonstrate their dedication to maintaining their expertise and upholding the highest standards of practice.

Organizations can play a pivotal role in supporting professional development and certification efforts among their workforces. By providing access to training resources, incentivizing certification attainment, and fostering a culture that values learning and development, companies can cultivate a highly skilled and motivated workforce. Investing in employee growth and development not only enhances organizational performance but also contributes to employee satisfaction, retention, and loyalty.

In conclusion, professional development and certification are essential components of continuous improvement in cost management. By investing in ongoing learning and credentialing initiatives, professionals can enhance their skills, advance their careers, and contribute to the overall success of their organizations. Embracing a culture of lifelong learning and professional growth is key to staying competitive and achieving excellence in cost management practices.

Cultivating a Culture of Continuous Improvement

A culture of continuous improvement is fundamental to driving excellence and innovation in cost management practices. This section explores the importance of fostering a culture that values learning, experimentation, and adaptability, and provides strategies for cultivating such a culture within organizations.

At the heart of a culture of continuous improvement lies a growth mindset—a belief that abilities and intelligence can be developed through dedication and effort. Organizations should encourage team members to view challenges as opportunities for growth, to embrace feedback and constructive criticism, and to persist in the face of setbacks. By cultivating a growth mindset, individuals are more likely to adopt a proactive approach to learning and improvement.

Empowering employees to take ownership of their work and to contribute ideas for improvement is essential for fostering a culture of continuous improvement. Organizations should create channels for employees to voice their suggestions, whether through suggestion boxes, brainstorming sessions, or dedicated improvement teams. By involving employees in the decision-making process and valuing their input, organizations tap into a wealth of collective knowledge and drive bottom-up innovation.

Risk-taking and experimentation are inherent to innovation and improvement. Organizations should create a safe environment where employees feel encouraged to try new approaches, experiment with different solutions, and learn from both successes and failures. By celebrating experimentation and acknowledging the value of learning from mistakes, organizations foster a culture of innovation and resilience.

To support continuous improvement efforts, organizations must provide employees with the resources, tools, and training necessary to succeed. This may include investing in training programs, providing access to learning resources, and offering mentorship and coaching opportunities. By equipping employees with the knowledge and skills they need to excel, organizations empower them to drive meaningful change and innovation.

Recognizing and celebrating achievements, no matter how small, is crucial for reinforcing a culture of continuous improvement. Organizations should acknowledge and reward individuals and teams for their contributions to improvement initiatives, whether through formal recognition programs, rewards, and incentives, or simply words of praise and appreciation. By celebrating progress and highlighting successes, organizations reinforce the importance of continuous improvement and motivate employees to continue their efforts.

In conclusion, cultivating a culture of continuous improvement is essential for driving excellence and innovation in cost management practices. By embracing a growth mindset, empowering employees, encouraging experimentation, providing resources and support, and recognizing and celebrating progress, organizations create an environment where learning and improvement thrive. By fostering a culture of continuous improvement, organizations can adapt to changing circumstances, drive innovation, and achieve long-term success in cost management.

Leveraging Technology for Continuous Improvement

Technology plays a pivotal role in enabling and accelerating continuous improvement initiatives in cost management. This section explores how organizations can harness technological advancements to drive efficiency, innovation, and excellence in cost management practices.

Utilizing Data Analytics for Insights

Data analytics tools and techniques enable organizations to gain valuable insights from vast amounts of data, empowering them to make informed decisions and drive continuous improvement.

By leveraging data analytics for cost analysis, organizations can identify patterns, trends, and areas for optimization, enabling them to enhance cost estimation accuracy, identify cost-saving opportunities, and improve budgeting and forecasting processes.

Implementing AI and Machine Learning

Artificial intelligence (AI) and machine learning (ML) technologies have the potential to revolutionize cost management practices by automating repetitive tasks, optimizing processes, and providing predictive insights. From automated cost estimation and budget allocation to predictive risk analysis and resource optimization, AI and ML enable organizations to streamline workflows, reduce manual effort, and make data-driven decisions, ultimately driving continuous improvement in cost management.

Adopting Project Management Software

Project management software solutions offer robust functionalities for planning, tracking, and managing project costs, schedules, and resources. By adopting integrated project management platforms, organizations can enhance collaboration, streamline communication, and improve visibility into project performance. Advanced features such as real-time reporting, resource allocation, and milestone tracking enable teams to identify bottlenecks, mitigate risks, and drive continuous improvement throughout the project lifecycle.

Implementing Building Information Modelling (BIM)

Building Information Modelling (BIM) technologies enable organizations to create digital representations of physical assets and simulate construction processes in a virtual environment. By integrating cost data into BIM models, organizations can perform cost analysis and optimization at every stage of the project lifecycle, from design and planning to construction and operation. BIM facilitates collaboration among stakeholders, enhances decision-making, and enables organizations to identify cost-saving opportunities and drive continuous improvement in cost management.

Leveraging Cloud Computing and Mobile Applications

Cloud computing and mobile applications offer organizations flexible and scalable solutions for accessing and managing cost-related data and resources. Cloud-based cost management platforms provide anytime, anywhere access to project information, enabling teams to collaborate in real-time and make data-driven decisions on the go. Mobile applications allow stakeholders to track project costs, monitor progress, and communicate effectively, driving efficiency and continuous improvement in cost management practices.

In conclusion, technology serves as a powerful enabler of continuous improvement in cost management practices. By harnessing data analytics, AI and ML, project management software, BIM, and cloud computing technologies, organizations can streamline processes, optimize resources, and make data-driven decisions to enhance cost management efficiency and effectiveness. By leveraging technology for continuous improvement, organizations can stay ahead of the curve, drive innovation, and achieve sustainable success in cost management.

Benchmarking and Best Practices

Benchmarking and adopting best practices are integral components of continuous improvement in cost management. This section explores the importance of benchmarking, identifies key best practices, and provides strategies for leveraging benchmarking data to drive ongoing improvement in cost management processes.

Benchmarking involves comparing an organization's cost management performance against industry standards, competitors, or internal benchmarks to identify areas for improvement and drive performance excellence. By benchmarking key cost metrics such as project costs, budget variances, and cost efficiency ratios, organizations gain valuable insights into their performance relative to peers and industry benchmarks, enabling them to identify opportunities for improvement and set realistic targets for improvement.

Key Best Practices in Cost Management

Several best practices can enhance cost management effectiveness and drive continuous improvement:

• **Cost Planning Excellence:** Develop comprehensive cost management plans that align with project objectives and business goals, ensuring accurate cost estimation, budgeting, and forecasting.

• **Risk Management Integration:** Integrate risk management processes into cost management practices to identify, assess, and mitigate cost-related risks proactively.

• **Change Control Discipline:** Implement robust change control processes to manage scope changes effectively, minimize cost overruns, and maintain project profitability.

• **Resource Optimization Strategies:** Optimize resource utilization and allocation to maximize efficiency, minimize waste, and enhance cost-effectiveness.

• **Performance Measurement and Monitoring:** Establish key performance indicators (KPIs) and metrics to track project costs, monitor performance, and identify deviations from planned targets.

• **Stakeholder Communication and Engagement:** Foster transparent communication and collaboration among project stakeholders to align expectations, address concerns, and ensure stakeholder satisfaction.

• **Continuous Improvement Culture:** Cultivate a culture of continuous improvement that encourages innovation, learning, and adaptation to drive excellence in cost management practices.

Leveraging Benchmarking Data for Improvement

To leverage benchmarking data effectively for continuous improvement, organizations should:

- **Identify Benchmarking Metrics:** Determine relevant cost management metrics to benchmark against industry standards, competitors, or internal benchmarks.

- **Collect Benchmarking Data:** Gather benchmarking data from reputable sources, industry associations, benchmarking databases, or through direct comparisons with competitors.

- **Analyse Benchmarking Data:** Analyse benchmarking data to identify performance gaps, trends, and best practices, and to gain insights into areas for improvement.

- **Develop Improvement Initiatives:** Develop improvement initiatives and action plans based on benchmarking findings to address performance gaps, implement best practices, and drive continuous improvement.

- **Monitor Progress and Adjust:** Continuously monitor progress against improvement initiatives, track performance metrics, and adjust strategies as needed to achieve desired outcomes and drive ongoing improvement.

In conclusion, benchmarking and adopting best practices are essential components of continuous improvement in cost management. By benchmarking key cost metrics, identifying best practices, and leveraging benchmarking data to drive improvement initiatives, organizations can enhance cost management effectiveness, optimize project performance, and achieve sustainable success. By embracing a culture of continuous improvement and learning, organizations can stay ahead of the curve, drive innovation, and maintain a competitive edge in today's dynamic business environment.

Continuous Improvement Frameworks and Models

Continuous improvement frameworks and models provide structured approaches for organizations to systematically identify, implement, and sustain improvements in cost management processes. These methodologies offer valuable tools and techniques to drive ongoing enhancement, foster innovation, and achieve excellence in cost management practices.

Continuous improvement frameworks offer systematic methodologies for driving ongoing improvement in organizational processes, including cost management. These frameworks provide structured approaches for identifying areas for improvement, implementing changes, and monitoring progress over time. By adopting continuous improvement frameworks, organizations can foster a culture of innovation and drive efficiency in cost management practices.

Several continuous improvement frameworks and models are widely used to enhance cost management effectiveness:

Lean Management: Lean principles focus on eliminating waste, optimizing processes, and maximizing value for customers. Techniques such as value stream mapping and Kaizen events help streamline cost management processes and reduce inefficiencies.

Six Sigma: Six Sigma methodologies aim to improve process quality and reduce variation by identifying and eliminating defects. Approaches like DMAIC or DMADV assist in enhancing cost management accuracy and optimizing cost performance.

Total Quality Management (TQM): TQM principles emphasize continuous improvement, customer focus, and employee involvement. Practices such as continuous training and customer feedback loops drive innovation in cost management.

Plan-Do-Check-Act (PDCA) Cycle: The PDCA cycle is a systematic approach for problem-solving and process improvement. By following steps of planning, implementing, evaluating, and adjusting, organizations can iteratively enhance cost management processes.

Balanced Scorecard: The Balanced Scorecard framework aligns strategic objectives with key performance indicators (KPIs) across multiple perspectives. It helps measure and track cost management performance holistically, driving continuous improvement.

To apply continuous improvement frameworks effectively in cost management, organizations should:

•   Assess Current State: Evaluate existing cost management processes to identify strengths, weaknesses, and areas for improvement.

•   Select Appropriate Framework: Choose the most suitable continuous improvement framework based on organizational needs, goals, and resources.

•   Define Improvement Goals: Establish clear objectives and targets for cost management improvement initiatives aligned with organizational priorities.

•   Implement Improvement Initiatives: Execute improvement initiatives systematically, leveraging tools and techniques provided by the selected framework.

•   Monitor and Measure Progress: Continuously monitor performance against improvement goals, track key metrics, and adjust strategies as needed.

•   Sustain Improvements: Embed continuous improvement practices into the organizational culture, fostering employee engagement, and ensuring ongoing commitment.

Continuous improvement frameworks offer valuable methodologies for enhancing cost management effectiveness, driving efficiency, and achieving excellence. By leveraging these approaches, organizations can optimize cost management processes, reduce waste, and drive sustainable improvement. Embracing a culture of continuous learning and improvement is essential for organizations to stay competitive, adapt to change, and achieve long-term success in cost management.

Monitoring and Measuring Continuous Improvement Efforts

Monitoring and measuring continuous improvement efforts are crucial aspects of effective cost management. This section explores the importance of tracking progress, evaluating performance, and ensuring that improvement initiatives yield desired outcomes.

Continuous improvement initiatives require systematic monitoring and measurement to gauge their effectiveness and impact on cost management processes. By closely tracking progress, organizations can identify areas of success, pinpoint areas needing improvement, and make data-driven decisions to drive ongoing enhancement.

Key Performance Indicators (KPIs)

Establishing key performance indicators (KPIs) is essential for monitoring and measuring continuous improvement efforts in cost management. These KPIs should align with organizational goals, reflect desired outcomes, and provide meaningful insights into the effectiveness of improvement initiatives. Common KPIs include:

• Cost Performance: Tracking cost variance, actual vs. budgeted costs, and cost savings achieved through improvement initiatives.

• Process Efficiency: Measuring cycle times, lead times, and process throughput to assess the efficiency of cost management processes.

• Quality Metrics: Monitoring error rates, defect rates, and customer satisfaction scores to evaluate the quality of cost management outputs.

• Employee Engagement: Assessing employee participation, feedback, and satisfaction with improvement efforts to gauge organizational commitment to continuous improvement.

Effective monitoring and measurement require robust data

collection and analysis processes. Organizations should collect relevant data points consistently, ensure data accuracy and integrity, and analyse data trends over time. By leveraging data analytics tools and techniques, organizations can uncover insights, identify patterns, and make informed decisions to drive continuous improvement.

Regular reviews and evaluations of continuous improvement initiatives are essential to assess progress, identify lessons learned, and adjust as needed. These reviews provide opportunities for stakeholders to discuss challenges, share best practices, and collaborate on strategies for further improvement. By fostering a culture of transparency and accountability, organizations can ensure that continuous improvement efforts remain on track and aligned with organizational objectives.

Effective communication of performance results is crucial for ensuring accountability, transparency, and organizational alignment. Organizations should develop clear and concise performance reports that highlight key achievements, challenges, and opportunities for improvement. These reports should be tailored to different stakeholders' needs and provide actionable insights to drive decision-making and action.

Monitoring and measuring continuous improvement efforts are essential for driving ongoing enhancement in cost management practices. By establishing relevant KPIs, implementing robust data collection and analysis processes, conducting regular reviews, and communicating performance results effectively, organizations can track progress, identify areas for improvement, and drive sustainable improvement in cost management processes. Embracing a culture of continuous improvement and accountability is key to achieving long-term success in cost management.

Overcoming Challenges in Continuous Improvement

Continuous improvement in cost management can face

various challenges that hinder progress and effectiveness. This section explores common obstacles and provides strategies for overcoming them to ensure successful continuous improvement efforts.

Identifying Common Challenges

1. **Resistance to Change:** Employee resistance to new processes or methodologies can impede continuous improvement efforts.

2. **Lack of Resources:** Inadequate budget, time, or personnel allocation may limit the organization's ability to implement improvement initiatives effectively.

3. **Limited Data Availability:** Insufficient data or poor data quality can hinder accurate performance measurement and analysis.

4. **Lack of Leadership Support:** Without strong leadership commitment and support, continuous improvement initiatives may struggle to gain traction and sustain momentum.

Strategies for Overcoming Challenges

1. **Employee Engagement and Training:** Foster a culture of continuous learning and improvement by involving employees in decision-making, providing training and development opportunities, and addressing concerns proactively.

2. **Resource Allocation:** Prioritize resources strategically, allocate sufficient budget, time, and personnel to improvement initiatives, and leverage cross-functional teams to maximize efficiency.

3. **Data Quality and Accessibility:** Invest in data collection and management systems, ensure data accuracy and integrity, and establish clear processes for data sharing and analysis.

4. **Leadership Buy-In and Communication:** Secure leadership buy-in early in the process, communicate the importance of continuous improvement, and lead by example to

inspire organizational commitment and engagement.

Continuous Improvement Frameworks

Implementing structured continuous improvement frameworks, such as Lean, Six Sigma, or Total Quality Management, can provide systematic approaches for addressing challenges and driving sustainable improvement in cost management practices.

Collaboration and Knowledge Sharing

Encourage collaboration and knowledge sharing across departments and organizational levels to leverage diverse perspectives, share best practices, and overcome challenges collectively.

Continuous Learning and Adaptation

Embrace a mindset of continuous learning and adaptation, encourage experimentation, and be open to feedback and course corrections along the journey of continuous improvement.

Overcoming challenges in continuous improvement requires proactive identification, strategic planning, and collaborative effort across the organization. By addressing resistance to change, allocating resources effectively, ensuring data quality, securing leadership support, and leveraging continuous improvement frameworks, organizations can overcome obstacles and drive sustainable improvement in cost management practices. Embracing a culture of collaboration, continuous learning, and adaptation is essential for overcoming challenges and achieving long-term success in continuous improvement efforts.

Throughout this chapter, we've traversed the landscape of continuous improvement in cost management, delving into its fundamental principles, challenges, and strategies.

We've learned that failures and cost overruns are not setbacks but opportunities for growth and learning. By dissecting these instances, organizations can extract valuable insights that serve as guideposts for future endeavours. Moreover, we've emphasized the importance of translating these lessons into actionable improvements, embedding them within organizational processes to foster resilience and adaptability.

Professional development emerges as a cornerstone in this journey, underscoring the need for ongoing education and certification to equip cost management professionals with the tools and knowledge necessary for success. By investing in talent and cultivating a culture that values learning, organizations can ensure a robust foundation for continuous improvement.

Technological advancements have revolutionized cost management, offering a plethora of tools and analytics to streamline processes and enhance decision-making. However, we've recognized that technology alone is not a panacea, its efficacy hinges on organizational readiness and alignment with strategic objectives.

In our exploration, collaboration and knowledge sharing emerged as catalysts for innovation and improvement. By fostering an environment where ideas flow freely and insights are shared across departments and hierarchical levels, organizations can harness collective intelligence to drive meaningful change.

As we conclude this chapter, we issue a call to action for organizations to embrace continuous improvement as a mindset, a culture, and a strategic imperative. By committing to ongoing learning, leveraging technology intelligently, and fostering a collaborative environment, organizations can navigate the complexities of cost management with confidence and agility, paving the way for sustained success in project budgeting and control.

CHAPTER 10: FUTURE TRENDS IN COST MANAGEMENT

As we navigate the ever-evolving landscape of project management, the importance of staying ahead of emerging trends in cost management cannot be overstated. The future of cost management promises to be shaped by advancements in technology, evolving regulatory standards, and the increasing emphasis on sustainability. To maintain a competitive edge and ensure the efficient allocation of resources, it is crucial for organizations and cost managers to anticipate and adapt to these changes.

Emerging technologies such as artificial intelligence (AI), blockchain, and the Internet of Things (IoT) are revolutionizing the way cost management is conducted. These innovations are not only enhancing the accuracy and efficiency of cost estimation and tracking but also enabling more proactive and data-driven decision-making processes. Understanding the potential impact of these technologies on cost management practices is essential for organizations aiming to leverage them effectively.

In addition to technological advancements, the regulatory environment surrounding cost management is also evolving. New regulations and compliance requirements are being introduced, driven by the need for greater transparency, accountability, and sustainability. Keeping abreast of these changes and understanding their implications is vital for ensuring that cost management practices align with current standards and industry best practices.

Sustainability is becoming a central focus in project management, and cost management is no exception. Integrating sustainable practices into cost management not only helps organizations meet regulatory requirements but also offers significant economic benefits. From green building initiatives to sustainable infrastructure projects, the shift towards sustainability is reshaping cost management strategies.

The future of cost management also demands a shift towards more agile and adaptive approaches. Traditional, rigid cost management methods are giving way to more flexible and dynamic strategies that can quickly respond to changing project conditions and stakeholder needs. Embracing these agile principles can enhance the resilience and effectiveness of cost management practices.

In this chapter, we will explore these future trends in detail, providing insights into how they are shaping the field of cost management. We will examine the emerging technologies driving change, the evolving regulatory and industry standards, the integration of sustainability, and the adoption of agile methodologies. Additionally, we will discuss the critical skills and competencies that future cost managers will need to thrive in this dynamic environment.

By understanding and preparing for these future trends, organizations can position themselves for success, ensuring that their cost management practices are not only current but also forward-thinking and innovative. This proactive approach will enable them to navigate the complexities of the modern project management landscape with confidence and efficiency.

Emerging Technologies and Their Impact on Cost Management

The future of cost management is poised for significant transformation, driven by the rapid adoption of emerging technologies. These technologies are revolutionizing traditional cost management practices, offering new levels of efficiency, accuracy, and insight. In this section, we will explore some of the key technological advancements and their profound impact on cost management.

Artificial Intelligence (AI) and Machine Learning (ML)

Artificial intelligence and machine learning are at the forefront of technological innovation in cost management. AI and ML algorithms can analyse vast amounts of data quickly and accurately, identifying patterns and predicting future cost trends with remarkable precision. These technologies enable cost managers to make more informed decisions, optimize resource allocation, and mitigate risks. For example, AI-driven predictive analytics can forecast potential cost overruns before they occur, allowing for proactive adjustments and more effective budgeting.

Blockchain Technology

Blockchain technology, known for its use in cryptocurrencies, is finding applications in cost management as well. Blockchain provides a secure and transparent ledger system that can track financial transactions and contractual agreements in real-time. This transparency reduces the risk of fraud and errors, ensuring that all parties involved in a project have access to accurate and immutable records. In construction and other industries with complex supply chains, blockchain can enhance accountability and streamline payment processes.

Internet of Things (IoT)

The Internet of Things (IoT) is transforming cost management by providing real-time data from interconnected devices and sensors. In construction, IoT devices can monitor equipment usage, track material consumption, and gather environmental data. This information helps project managers optimize resource utilization, reduce waste, and control costs more effectively. IoT-enabled smart buildings can also provide data on energy usage, enabling better cost control and sustainability measures.

Big Data and Data Analytics

The rise of big data has revolutionized cost management by enabling the analysis of large and complex datasets. Advanced data analytics tools can extract meaningful insights from these datasets, helping organizations identify cost-saving opportunities and inefficiencies. For instance, data analytics can reveal trends in labour costs, material prices, and project timelines, allowing for more accurate cost estimations and better decision-making.

Building Information Modelling (BIM)

Building Information Modelling (BIM) is a game-changer in the construction industry, offering a digital representation of a building's physical and functional characteristics. BIM integrates all aspects of a project, from design to construction to operation, in a single digital model. This integration allows for more accurate cost estimation, improved collaboration among stakeholders, and better project management. By visualizing potential issues before they arise, BIM reduces costly rework and delays.

Robotics and Automation

Robotics and automation are streamlining various aspects of project management and cost control. In construction, robots can perform repetitive tasks such as bricklaying and concrete pouring with greater speed and precision than human workers. Automation tools can also manage routine administrative tasks, freeing up cost managers to focus on more strategic activities. The use of drones for site surveys and inspections provides real-time data, improving accuracy and reducing the time and cost associated with manual inspections.

Cloud Computing

Cloud computing offers scalable and flexible solutions for cost management. Cloud-based platforms allow for real-time collaboration and data sharing among project teams, regardless of their physical location. This accessibility ensures that all stakeholders have up-to-date information, facilitating better decision-making and cost control. Cloud computing also supports the use of advanced analytics and AI tools, further enhancing cost management capabilities.

Augmented Reality (AR) and Virtual Reality (VR)

Augmented Reality (AR) and Virtual Reality (VR) are transforming the way projects are visualised and managed. AR can overlay digital information onto the physical world, providing cost managers with real-time data on project progress and potential issues. VR offers immersive simulations of project environments, allowing for virtual walkthroughs and detailed cost analysis. These technologies enhance communication and collaboration, reducing the likelihood of costly misunderstandings.

The integration of these emerging technologies into cost management practices is not without challenges. Organizations must invest in the necessary infrastructure and training to fully leverage these tools. Additionally, the rapid pace of technological advancement requires ongoing adaptation and learning.

In conclusion, the impact of emerging technologies on cost management is profound and far-reaching. By embracing AI, blockchain, IoT, big data, BIM, robotics, cloud computing, AR, and VR, organizations can achieve greater efficiency, accuracy, and insight in their cost management processes. Staying ahead of these technological trends is essential for maintaining a competitive edge and ensuring the successful completion of projects within budget.

Evolving Regulatory and Industry Standards

As the landscape of cost management continues to evolve, so do the regulatory and industry standards that govern it. Keeping abreast of these changes is critical for organizations aiming to maintain compliance, optimize their processes, and achieve long-term success. This section delves into the dynamic nature of regulatory requirements and industry standards, highlighting their implications for cost management.

Regulatory Frameworks and Compliance

The regulatory environment for cost management is becoming increasingly complex. Governments and regulatory bodies worldwide are continually updating laws and regulations to enhance transparency, accountability, and sustainability in project management. Key areas of focus include financial reporting, environmental impact, labour practices, and data security.

For instance, financial reporting standards such as the International Financial Reporting Standards (IFRS) and the Generally Accepted Accounting Principles (GAAP) provide guidelines for accurate and consistent cost reporting. Compliance with these standards ensures that financial statements are transparent and comparable, facilitating better decision-making and investor confidence.

Environmental regulations are also tightening, with governments imposing stricter guidelines on emissions, waste management, and resource usage. Adhering to these regulations often requires significant investments in sustainable practices and technologies, but it also opens up opportunities for cost savings through increased efficiency and reduced environmental impact.

Industry Standards and Best Practices

In addition to regulatory requirements, industry standards

play a crucial role in shaping cost management practices. Organizations such as the Project Management Institute (PMI) and the International Project Management Association (IPMA) provide frameworks and guidelines that help standardize project management processes, including cost management.

The PMI's Project Management Body of Knowledge (PMBOK) and the IPMA's Individual Competence Baseline (ICB) are widely recognized standards that outline best practices for cost estimation, budgeting, and control. These standards emphasize the importance of integrating cost management with other project management processes, such as scope, time, and quality management.

Adhering to industry standards not only ensures consistency and quality in cost management practices but also enhances an organization's reputation and credibility. It demonstrates a commitment to excellence and continuous improvement, which can be a key differentiator in competitive markets.

Sustainability and Corporate Social Responsibility (CSR) Standards

Sustainability and CSR are becoming increasingly important in the realm of cost management. Standards such as the Global Reporting Initiative (GRI) and the Sustainability Accounting Standards Board (SASB) provide frameworks for reporting on environmental, social, and governance (ESG) performance.

These standards encourage organizations to consider the broader impact of their projects on society and the environment. Integrating ESG considerations into cost management can lead to more sustainable and responsible business practices, aligning with stakeholder expectations and regulatory requirements.

For example, the GRI standards provide guidelines for reporting on resource usage, emissions, and waste management, while the SASB standards focus on industry-specific sustainability issues. By adhering to these standards, organizations can enhance their transparency and accountability, build trust with stakeholders, and mitigate risks associated with non-compliance.

Technological Advancements and Regulatory Adaptation

As technological advancements reshape cost management practices, regulatory bodies are also adapting to these changes. For instance, the increasing use of blockchain technology for secure and transparent financial transactions is prompting regulators to develop new guidelines and frameworks for its use.

Similarly, the rise of artificial intelligence and machine learning in cost management is leading to discussions about ethical considerations and data privacy. Regulators are exploring ways to ensure that these technologies are used responsibly, and that data is protected from misuse and breaches.

Organizations must stay informed about these evolving regulatory requirements and industry standards to remain compliant and competitive. This involves regularly reviewing and updating their cost management processes, investing in training and development, and leveraging technology to streamline compliance efforts.

Globalization and Harmonization of Standards

The globalization of business is driving the harmonization of regulatory and industry standards across different regions. International bodies such as the International Organization for Standardization (ISO) are working towards creating unified standards that facilitate cross-border trade and collaboration.

For example, the ISO 21500 standard provides guidelines for project management, including cost management, which are applicable globally. By adopting such standards, organizations can ensure consistency in their cost management practices, regardless of the geographical location of their projects.

In conclusion, the evolving regulatory and industry standards in cost management are shaping the way organizations plan, execute, and report on their projects. Staying ahead of these changes requires a proactive approach to compliance, continuous improvement, and leveraging technology to streamline processes. By aligning with these standards, organizations can enhance their transparency, accountability, and sustainability, ultimately driving long-term success and competitiveness.

Sustainability and Green Cost Management

In the contemporary business environment, sustainability and green cost management are no longer optional but essential for long-term success and competitiveness. This section explores the integration of sustainable practices into cost management, highlighting the financial, environmental, and social benefits of green cost management strategies.

Sustainability in cost management involves incorporating environmental and social considerations into the financial planning and execution of projects. This holistic approach aims to reduce negative impacts on the environment and society while still achieving economic objectives. Sustainable cost management practices are designed to enhance resource efficiency, minimize waste, and promote responsible use of materials.

Benefits of Green Cost Management

Integrating sustainability into cost management offers numerous benefits. Environmentally friendly practices can lead to significant cost savings through improved efficiency and reduced waste. For example, energy-efficient buildings and equipment lower utility costs, while recycling and reusing materials can reduce procurement expenses.

Moreover, sustainability initiatives can enhance an organization's reputation and brand value. Companies that demonstrate a commitment to sustainability attract socially conscious consumers, investors, and employees. This positive image can lead to increased sales, investment, and employee satisfaction, ultimately contributing to the bottom line.

Key Strategies for Green Cost Management

1. **Life Cycle Cost Analysis (LCCA):** LCCA is a critical tool in green cost management, helping organizations evaluate the total cost of ownership over the life of an asset. By considering initial costs, operation, maintenance, and disposal costs, LCCA ensures that sustainable choices are cost-effective in the long run. For instance, investing in energy-efficient systems may have higher upfront costs but result in lower operating expenses and a smaller carbon footprint over time.

2. **Sustainable Design and Construction:** Adopting sustainable design principles, such as using renewable materials and incorporating natural lighting, can significantly reduce environmental impact and operational costs. Green building certifications like LEED (Leadership in Energy and Environmental Design) provide frameworks for implementing sustainable practices in construction and operations.

3. **Resource Optimization:** Efficient use of resources is a cornerstone of green cost management. Techniques such as just-in-time inventory management and predictive maintenance can minimize waste and optimize resource utilization. This not only reduces costs but also lessens the environmental impact by minimizing resource extraction and waste generation.

4. **Renewable Energy Integration:** Transitioning to renewable energy sources, such as solar or wind power, can lead to substantial cost savings and reduced greenhouse gas emissions. While the initial investment may be high, the long-term benefits include lower energy bills, tax incentives, and enhanced energy security.

Challenges and Solutions in Implementing Green Cost Management

Implementing sustainable practices in cost management presents several challenges, including higher upfront costs, resistance to change, and lack of awareness or expertise. Overcoming these obstacles requires a strategic approach:

- **Education and Training:** Raising awareness and building expertise in sustainable practices among employees and stakeholders is crucial. This can be achieved through training programs, workshops, and sustainability initiatives.

- **Stakeholder Engagement:** Engaging stakeholders, including suppliers, customers, and investors, in sustainability efforts ensures broad-based support and collaboration. Transparent communication about the benefits and progress of sustainability initiatives can foster a culture of shared responsibility.

- **Incentives and Support:** Governments and industry bodies often provide incentives, grants, and support for adopting sustainable practices. Organizations should actively seek out and leverage these opportunities to offset initial costs and gain competitive advantages.

Future Outlook of Green Cost Management

The future of green cost management looks promising, with increasing emphasis on sustainability from consumers, investors, and regulatory bodies. Advances in technology, such as smart grids and IoT-enabled energy management systems, will further facilitate the adoption of green practices. Additionally, evolving regulations will likely mandate higher standards of environmental performance, making green cost management an integral part of business strategy.

In conclusion, integrating sustainability into cost management is not only beneficial for the environment and society but also makes sound financial sense. Organizations that embrace green cost management strategies are better positioned to achieve long-term success, enhance their reputation, and contribute positively to global sustainability goals. By leveraging tools like LCCA, adopting sustainable design principles, and optimizing resource use, companies can create value for all stakeholders while minimizing their environmental footprint.

Agile and Adaptive Cost Management Approaches

In an increasingly dynamic business environment, traditional cost management methods often fall short in addressing the rapid changes and uncertainties faced by modern projects. This is where agile and adaptive cost management approaches come into play, offering a more flexible, responsive framework for managing costs in real-time.

Understanding Agile Cost Management

Agile cost management is rooted in the principles of agile project management, which emphasizes iterative progress, collaboration, and flexibility. Unlike traditional methods that rely on fixed budgets and rigid plans, agile cost management allows for continuous adjustment and real-time responsiveness to changing project conditions. This approach is particularly beneficial for projects characterized by high uncertainty, fast-paced changes, and innovative processes.

Key Components of Agile Cost Management

1. **Iterative Budgeting and Forecasting:** Agile cost management involves breaking down the project budget into smaller, manageable increments that are reviewed and adjusted regularly. This iterative process allows project managers to respond swiftly to any changes in scope, market conditions, or unforeseen challenges, ensuring that resources are allocated efficiently and effectively.

2. **Continuous Feedback and Improvement:** Regular feedback loops are integral to agile cost management. By continuously monitoring project performance and gathering feedback from stakeholders, project teams can identify areas for cost optimization and make necessary adjustments promptly. This ongoing process helps in maintaining financial control and maximizing value delivery.

3. **Collaborative Decision-Making:** Agile cost management fosters a collaborative environment where cross-functional teams work together to manage costs. This collaborative approach ensures that cost-related decisions are informed by

diverse perspectives and expertise, leading to more balanced and effective financial management.

Adaptive Cost Management Strategies

Adaptive cost management complements agile methods by focusing on the ability to adjust and optimize cost management strategies in response to evolving project dynamics. It emphasizes flexibility, proactive risk management, and strategic foresight.

1. **Scenario Planning and Analysis:** Adaptive cost management involves preparing for multiple scenarios and developing contingency plans. By anticipating potential risks and opportunities, project managers can create flexible budgets that accommodate different outcomes, ensuring preparedness for any eventuality.

2. **Risk-Based Cost Management:** Identifying and prioritizing risks is crucial in adaptive cost management. By assessing the likelihood and impact of various risks, project managers can allocate resources strategically to mitigate high-priority risks and capitalize on opportunities, thereby maintaining financial stability and project resilience.

3. **Dynamic Resource Allocation:** Adaptive cost management requires the ability to reallocate resources swiftly based on project needs and priorities. This dynamic allocation ensures that resources are directed to the most critical areas, enhancing efficiency and effectiveness in cost management.

Benefits of Agile and Adaptive Cost Management

The agile and adaptive approaches to cost management offer several advantages:

- **Enhanced Flexibility:** These methods provide the flexibility to respond quickly to changes, ensuring that cost management strategies remain relevant and effective throughout the project lifecycle.

- **Improved Efficiency:** By continuously optimizing

resource allocation and adjusting budgets in real-time, agile, and adaptive cost management enhance overall project efficiency and cost-effectiveness.

• **Greater Stakeholder Engagement:** The collaborative nature of these approaches fosters greater stakeholder involvement, leading to more informed and balanced cost-related decisions.

• **Risk Mitigation:** Proactive risk management and scenario planning help in identifying potential issues early, allowing for timely interventions and minimizing financial risks.

Implementing Agile and Adaptive Cost Management

To implement agile and adaptive cost management successfully, organizations need to embrace a cultural shift towards flexibility and continuous improvement. This involves:

• **Training and Development:** Investing in training programs to equip project teams with the skills and knowledge required for agile and adaptive cost management.

• **Technology Integration:** Leveraging advanced project management tools and software that support iterative budgeting, real-time monitoring, and dynamic resource allocation.

• **Leadership Support:** Ensuring strong leadership support to drive the adoption of agile and adaptive cost management practices and foster a culture of collaboration and innovation.

Challenges and Solutions

While agile and adaptive cost management offer significant benefits, they also present challenges such as resistance to change, the need for continuous learning, and the complexity of managing dynamic budgets. Addressing these challenges requires a strategic approach:

• **Change Management:** Implementing effective change

management strategies to address resistance and facilitate the transition to agile and adaptive methods.

• **Continuous Learning:** Promoting a culture of continuous learning and improvement to ensure that project teams remain adaptable and responsive to evolving project demands.

• **Simplifying Processes:** Streamlining cost management processes to reduce complexity and enhance ease of implementation.

In conclusion, agile and adaptive cost management approaches provide a robust framework for managing costs in an ever-changing project environment. By embracing flexibility, collaboration, and continuous improvement, organizations can enhance their cost management capabilities, ensuring that they remain responsive and resilient in the face of uncertainties and dynamic market conditions.

The Role of Big Data in Cost Management

As we move further into the digital age, the role of big data in cost management is becoming increasingly significant. The sheer volume, velocity, and variety of data generated in today's business environment present both challenges and opportunities for cost management. Harnessing the power of big data can lead to more accurate forecasting, better decision-making, and enhanced efficiency in managing costs.

Understanding Big Data in Cost Management

Big data refers to large and complex datasets that traditional data processing tools find challenging to handle. In cost management, big data encompasses all the financial, operational, and transactional data generated within an organization. This data can be structured, such as financial statements and budgets, or unstructured, like emails and social media interactions.

Key Applications of Big Data in Cost Management

1. **Enhanced Forecasting and Budgeting**

Big data analytics allows organizations to create more accurate forecasts and budgets by analysing historical data, market trends, and other relevant variables. Advanced algorithms can process vast amounts of data to identify patterns and correlations that would be impossible to detect manually. This results in more precise predictions of future costs and revenues, leading to better financial planning.

2. **Real-Time Cost Monitoring**

The ability to monitor costs in real-time is one of the most significant advantages of big data in cost management. By integrating data from various sources, organizations can track expenses as they occur and compare them against budgets and forecasts. This real-time visibility enables prompt identification of cost overruns and allows for immediate corrective actions.

3. **Predictive Analytics for Risk Management**

Predictive analytics, powered by big data, can identify potential risks before they become significant issues. By analysing data from past projects, current market conditions, and other risk factors, organizations can predict where cost overruns or inefficiencies are likely to occur. This proactive approach helps in mitigating risks and optimizing resource allocation.

4. **Optimization of Resource Allocation**

Big data can help organizations optimize resource allocation by providing detailed insights into where and how resources are being used. Analysing data on labour, materials, and equipment usage can highlight inefficiencies and areas for improvement. This ensures that resources are allocated where they are needed most, maximizing productivity, and minimizing waste.

5. **Improved Supplier and Vendor Management**

Big data analytics can enhance supplier and vendor management by providing insights into supplier performance, pricing trends, and contract compliance. Organizations can use this information to negotiate better terms, identify reliable suppliers, and manage supplier relationships more effectively. This leads to cost savings and improved procurement processes.

Challenges in Leveraging Big Data for Cost Management

While the benefits of big data in cost management are substantial, there are several challenges that organizations must address to harness its full potential:

• **Data Quality and Integration:** Ensuring the quality and consistency of data from various sources is critical. Organizations must invest in robust data integration and cleaning processes to avoid inaccuracies that can lead to poor decision-making.

• **Data Security and Privacy:** With the increased use of big data comes heightened concerns about data security and privacy. Organizations must implement stringent security measures to protect sensitive financial data from breaches and ensure compliance with data protection regulations.

• **Skill Gaps:** The effective use of big data requires specialized skills in data analytics and interpretation. Organizations may face challenges in finding and retaining professionals with the necessary expertise. Investing in training and development is essential to build a capable workforce.

• **Cost and Infrastructure:** Implementing big data solutions can be costly, requiring significant investments in technology and infrastructure. Organizations need to carefully consider the cost-benefit ratio and ensure that the investment aligns with their strategic goals.

Best Practices for Implementing Big Data in Cost Management

To successfully leverage big data in cost management, organizations should consider the following best practices:

• **Develop a Clear Strategy:** Establish a clear strategy for how big data will be used in cost management. This includes defining objectives, identifying key data sources, and determining the metrics for success.

• **Invest in the Right Tools:** Choose advanced analytics tools and software that can handle large datasets and provide meaningful insights. Cloud-based solutions can offer scalability and flexibility, making them a good option for many organizations.

• **Foster a Data-Driven Culture:** Encourage a data-driven culture within the organization where decision-making is based on data insights rather than intuition. This requires buy-in from leadership and continuous education and training for employees.

• **Ensure Data Governance:** Implement robust data governance policies to ensure data quality, security, and compliance. This includes establishing data standards, creating data ownership roles, and regularly auditing data practices.

• **Collaborate Across Departments:** Cost management involves multiple departments, including finance, operations, and procurement. Promote collaboration across these departments to ensure that data is shared and utilized effectively.

Future Outlook for Big Data in Cost Management

As technology continues to evolve, the role of big data in cost management is set to expand further. The integration of artificial intelligence and machine learning with big data analytics will enable even more sophisticated forecasting and decision-making capabilities. Additionally, advancements in real-time data processing and the Internet of Things (IoT) will provide unprecedented visibility into costs and operations, leading to more efficient and effective cost management practices.

In conclusion, big data offers transformative potential for cost management by enhancing forecasting, improving resource allocation, and enabling real-time cost monitoring. By addressing the challenges and adopting best practices, organizations can harness the power of big data to achieve greater efficiency, cost savings, and strategic advantage.

Integration of Cost Management with Other Business Functions

The integration of cost management with other business functions is a crucial trend shaping the future of effective project budgeting and control. In today's interconnected and dynamic business environment, cost management can no longer operate in isolation. Instead, it must be seamlessly integrated with various functions such as operations, procurement, human resources, and strategic planning to enhance overall organizational performance and achieve business goals.

Integrating cost management with operations is fundamental to optimizing efficiency and productivity. Operations involve the day-to-day activities that contribute directly to the production of goods and services. By aligning cost management processes with operational activities, organizations can ensure that resources are used efficiently, and wastage is minimized.

For example, real-time cost tracking and analysis can provide valuable insights into operational efficiencies, allowing managers to identify areas where costs can be reduced without compromising on quality or output. Additionally, integrating cost management with production scheduling and inventory management can help in maintaining optimal stock levels, reducing carrying costs, and avoiding production delays.

Procurement and supply chain management are critical areas where cost management plays a significant role. Effective integration of these functions can lead to substantial cost savings and improved supplier relationships. By incorporating cost management strategies into procurement processes, organizations can negotiate better terms with suppliers, ensure competitive pricing, and manage contracts more effectively.

Moreover, a collaborative approach between cost management and supply chain management can enhance transparency and traceability throughout the supply chain. This enables organizations to identify cost drivers at each stage, optimize logistics, and implement just-in-time inventory practices, all of which contribute to cost efficiency.

Human resources (HR) are another key area where cost management integration can yield significant benefits. Labor costs often constitute a substantial portion of a project's budget, making it essential to align HR practices with cost management objectives. By integrating these functions, organizations can achieve a balance between managing labour costs and maintaining employee satisfaction and productivity.

For instance, workforce planning and cost management can be synchronized to ensure that staffing levels align with project needs and budget constraints. Additionally, integrating cost management with employee training and development programs can help in optimizing the allocation of training resources and measuring the return on investment in human capital.

Strategic planning and financial management are inherently linked with cost management. Integrating these functions ensures that cost management aligns with the organization's long-term goals and financial objectives. This integration facilitates comprehensive financial planning, budgeting, and forecasting, enabling organizations to make informed decisions based on a holistic view of their financial health.

Through integrated financial systems, organizations can streamline budget preparation, track expenditures against forecasts, and perform variance analysis to identify discrepancies and take corrective actions. This strategic alignment also supports the evaluation of investment opportunities, cost-benefit analysis, and the management of financial risks.

The integration of cost management with technology and IT functions is pivotal in leveraging technological advancements to enhance cost efficiency. By adopting integrated software solutions and digital tools, organizations can automate cost management processes, improve data accuracy, and gain real-time insights into financial performance.

For example, integrating enterprise resource planning (ERP) systems with cost management software enables seamless data flow between different business functions, providing a unified view of costs across the organization. This integration supports advanced analytics, predictive modelling, and scenario analysis, empowering organizations to make data-driven decisions.

Marketing and sales functions also benefit from integration with cost management. Understanding the cost implications of marketing campaigns and sales strategies helps organizations allocate budgets effectively and maximize return on investment. By integrating cost management with customer relationship management (CRM) systems, organizations can analyse the cost of acquiring and retaining customers, optimize pricing strategies, and enhance profitability.

Moreover, collaboration between cost management and marketing teams can lead to more accurate product costing and pricing decisions. This integration ensures that pricing strategies reflect true costs, market conditions, and competitive dynamics, ultimately supporting sustainable revenue growth.

The integration of cost management with other business functions represents a holistic approach to achieving organizational efficiency and financial sustainability. By breaking down silos and fostering collaboration across functions, organizations can optimize resource utilization, enhance decision-making, and drive continuous improvement.

In conclusion, the future of cost management lies in its ability to integrate seamlessly with various business functions. This integration not only enhances the accuracy and effectiveness of cost management processes but also supports overall business performance and strategic objectives. As organizations continue to embrace digital transformation and adopt integrated systems, the alignment of cost management with other functions will become increasingly critical in navigating the complexities of the modern business landscape.

Remote Work and Its Influence on Cost Management

The rise of remote work has fundamentally transformed the landscape of cost management in organizations. As businesses adapt to this new mode of operation, understanding its impact on costs is crucial for effective project budgeting and control. Remote work introduces both opportunities and challenges, influencing various cost components and necessitating adjustments in cost management strategies.

Reduction in Overhead Costs

One of the most significant impacts of remote work is the reduction in overhead costs. With fewer employees working on-site, organizations can reduce expenditures related to office space, utilities, maintenance, and office supplies. This reduction in overhead can lead to substantial cost savings, which can be redirected to other strategic initiatives or used to improve profitability.

For example, companies can downsize their office spaces, opting for smaller, more flexible workspaces that accommodate a hybrid workforce. Additionally, reduced utility costs from lower energy consumption in office buildings can further contribute to cost savings. These changes require cost managers to reevaluate budget allocations and forecast future savings accurately.

Technology and Infrastructure Investments

While remote work reduces certain costs, it also necessitates increased investments in technology and infrastructure.

Organizations must ensure that remote employees have access to the necessary tools and resources to perform their duties effectively. This includes investments in laptops, software licenses, virtual private networks (VPNs), and secure communication platforms.

Moreover, to support a distributed workforce, companies need to enhance their cybersecurity measures, implement robust IT support systems, and provide training for employees on remote work best practices. These technology-related expenditures must be carefully planned and managed to balance cost efficiency with the need for effective remote work infrastructure.

Impact on Human Resources Costs

Remote work influences human resources (HR) costs in various ways. While there may be savings related to reduced on-site amenities and travel expenses, organizations might need to invest more in employee engagement, well-being programs, and remote work stipends. Ensuring that remote employees remain productive, motivated, and connected to the company culture requires thoughtful HR strategies and potential financial investment.

Additionally, remote work enables organizations to tap into a global talent pool, potentially reducing labour costs by hiring in regions with lower wage rates. However, this also introduces complexities related to managing a diverse and geographically dispersed workforce, including considerations for varying labour laws, tax implications, and compensation structures.

Changes in Operational Costs

Remote work can lead to changes in operational costs related to project management and collaboration. Traditional in-person meetings and workshops may be replaced by virtual meetings, which can reduce travel and accommodation expenses. However, organizations need to invest in effective collaboration tools and platforms to maintain productivity and communication among remote teams.

Project management practices may also need to be adjusted to account for the challenges of remote work, such as coordinating across different time zones and ensuring accountability. These adjustments may incur costs related to training, process redesign, and the implementation of new project management tools.

Impact on Productivity and Performance Measurement

The impact of remote work on productivity varies across organizations and industries. While some companies report increased productivity due to flexible work arrangements, others face challenges related to employee engagement and collaboration. Accurately measuring and managing productivity in a remote work environment requires new approaches and metrics.

Organizations may need to invest in performance management systems that provide real-time data and insights into employee productivity and project progress. These systems can help identify areas where remote work is successful and where improvements are needed. Cost managers must consider the costs associated with these systems and the potential return on investment in terms of enhanced productivity.

Adapting Cost Management Strategies

The shift to remote work necessitates a re-evaluation of traditional cost management strategies. Organizations must adopt more flexible and adaptive approaches to budgeting and cost control, considering the dynamic nature of remote work arrangements. This includes regularly reviewing and adjusting budgets to reflect changes in workforce composition, technology needs, and operational requirements.

Cost managers should also focus on developing strategies to mitigate risks associated with remote work, such as cybersecurity threats and compliance issues. By proactively identifying and addressing these risks, organizations can avoid potential cost overruns and ensure the sustainability of remote work practices.

Embracing the New Normal

The influence of remote work on cost management is profound and multifaceted. As remote work becomes an integral part of the modern business environment, organizations must embrace this new normal by adapting their cost management practices accordingly. By recognizing the cost implications of remote work and making strategic investments in technology, infrastructure, and human resources, companies can optimize their budgets and enhance overall efficiency.

In conclusion, remote work presents both opportunities and challenges for cost management. By understanding and addressing these impacts, organizations can achieve cost savings, improve productivity, and maintain a competitive edge in an increasingly remote and digital world. The future of cost management will undoubtedly be shaped by the continued evolution of remote work and the ability of organizations to adapt to this transformative trend.

Future Skills and Competencies for Cost Managers

As the landscape of cost management evolves, the skills and competencies required for cost managers are also changing. The future of cost management will demand a combination of traditional expertise and new capabilities driven by technological advancements, sustainability considerations, and increasingly complex project environments. This section explores the critical skills and competencies that will define the next generation of cost managers.

Technological Proficiency

In the era of digital transformation, technological proficiency is no longer optional for cost managers. Proficiency in advanced cost management software, data analytics tools, and enterprise resource planning (ERP) systems is essential. Cost managers must be adept at leveraging these technologies to streamline processes, enhance accuracy, and generate insightful reports.

Familiarity with emerging technologies such as artificial intelligence (AI) and machine learning (ML) will also be crucial. These technologies can automate routine tasks, predict cost trends, and provide actionable insights through data analysis. Understanding how to integrate and use these tools effectively will enable cost managers to stay ahead of the curve.

Data Analytics and Business Intelligence

Data analytics and business intelligence are at the forefront of modern cost management. Future cost managers must be skilled in collecting, analysing, and interpreting vast amounts of data to make informed decisions. This involves not only understanding the data but also using it to identify trends, forecast future costs, and optimize budget allocations.

Competence in statistical analysis and familiarity with data visualization tools are essential. Cost managers should be able to present data in a clear and compelling manner, making it accessible to stakeholders at all levels. This skill will be vital in driving strategic decision-making and demonstrating the value of cost management initiatives.

Sustainability and Green Cost Management

As sustainability becomes a central concern for businesses, cost managers must develop expertise in sustainable cost management practices. This includes understanding the cost implications of environmentally friendly initiatives and integrating environmental and social costs into project budgeting.

Knowledge of life cycle cost analysis (LCCA) and sustainable procurement practices will be important. Cost managers will need to assess the long-term cost savings and benefits of sustainable practices, balancing them against initial expenditures. This competency will be critical in helping organizations achieve their sustainability goals while maintaining financial performance.

Risk Management

Effective risk management is a cornerstone of successful cost management. Future cost managers must be proficient in identifying, assessing, and mitigating cost-related risks. This involves a deep understanding of risk management frameworks and the ability to develop strategies that protect the organization from financial uncertainties.

In addition to traditional risk management skills, cost managers should be able to leverage predictive analytics to anticipate potential risks. By using data-driven insights, they can proactively address issues before they escalate, ensuring projects stay within budget and on schedule.

Agile and Adaptive Project Management

The dynamic nature of modern projects requires cost managers to be agile and adaptive. Familiarity with agile project management methodologies, such as Scrum and Kanban, will be increasingly valuable. These approaches emphasize flexibility, continuous improvement, and collaboration, enabling cost managers to respond swiftly to changing project requirements and constraints.

Adaptive cost management also involves iterative planning and regular feedback loops. Cost managers should be skilled in adjusting budgets and forecasts in response to new information and shifting project landscapes. This adaptability will be crucial in managing complex and fast-paced projects effectively.

Strategic Thinking and Decision-Making

Strategic thinking is essential for aligning cost management practices with broader business goals. Future cost managers must be capable of seeing the bigger picture, understanding how cost decisions impact the organization's overall strategy, and contributing to long-term success.

This requires strong analytical skills, the ability to evaluate different scenarios, and the foresight to anticipate future trends. Cost managers should be adept at making data-driven decisions that balance short-term needs with long-term objectives, ensuring sustainable growth and competitiveness.

Communication and Stakeholder Engagement

Effective communication is a vital skill for cost managers, who must convey complex financial information to a diverse range of stakeholders. This includes senior executives, project managers, and team members, each with varying levels of financial literacy.

Future cost managers should excel in both written and verbal communication, capable of presenting cost reports and analysis in a clear and compelling manner. Strong interpersonal skills are also necessary for building relationships, negotiating with vendors, and collaborating with cross-functional teams. Engaging stakeholders and ensuring they understand, and support cost management initiatives will be key to successful project outcomes.

Continuous Learning and Professional Development

The field of cost management is continuously evolving, driven by technological advancements, regulatory changes, and industry trends. Future cost managers must commit to lifelong learning and professional development to stay current with best practices and emerging tools.

This involves pursuing advanced certifications, attending industry conferences, and participating in professional organizations. Keeping abreast of the latest developments in cost management, finance, and technology will enable cost managers to maintain their expertise and provide the highest level of value to their organizations.

Preparing for the Future

The future of cost management will be shaped by a combination of traditional expertise and new competencies driven by technological and industry trends. By developing skills in technology, data analytics, sustainability, risk management, agile methodologies, strategic thinking, communication, and continuous learning, future cost managers will be well-equipped to navigate the complexities of modern project environments.

As organizations increasingly recognize the strategic importance of cost management, the role of the cost manager will continue to evolve. Those who embrace these future skills and competencies will not only excel in their careers but also drive their organizations toward greater efficiency, sustainability, and success.

Cybersecurity and Risk Management

In an increasingly digital world, cybersecurity has emerged as a critical component of risk management in cost management practices. This section delves into the intersection of cybersecurity and cost management, highlighting the importance of safeguarding financial data and mitigating cyber threats.

As cost management processes become more reliant on digital systems and data analytics tools, the risk of cyber threats escalates. Cost managers must recognize the potential vulnerabilities in their technology infrastructure, including financial databases, project management software, and communication platforms. Cyber threats such as data breaches, ransomware attacks, and phishing scams pose significant risks to financial data integrity and confidentiality. Understanding the nature of these threats is the first step in implementing effective cybersecurity measures.

To address cybersecurity risks effectively, cost managers

must integrate cybersecurity considerations into their cost management practices. This involves implementing robust cybersecurity protocols and controls to protect sensitive financial information from unauthorized access or exploitation. Encryption, multi-factor authentication, and regular system updates are essential measures for safeguarding financial data. Moreover, cost managers should establish clear policies and procedures for handling financial transactions and sensitive data to minimize the risk of cyber incidents.

In addition to protecting financial data from external threats, cost managers must also ensure compliance with data privacy regulations such as the General Data Protection Regulation (GDPR) and the California Consumer Privacy Act (CCPA). These regulations impose strict requirements on the collection, storage, and processing of personal and financial data, necessitating enhanced data privacy measures. Cost managers should prioritize data encryption, anonymization, and pseudonymization to uphold data privacy principles and mitigate the risk of regulatory penalties.

Cybersecurity is not solely a technological issue; it also requires a human-centric approach. Cost managers should invest in cybersecurity training and awareness programs to educate employees about cyber threats and best practices for mitigating them. Employee awareness is critical in preventing cyber incidents such as phishing attacks and social engineering scams, which often exploit human vulnerabilities. By fostering a culture of cybersecurity awareness, organizations can empower employees to identify and report potential threats promptly, enhancing overall cybersecurity resilience.

Effective cybersecurity requires collaboration between cost management teams and IT security professionals. Cost managers should work closely with IT security teams to identify vulnerabilities, assess risks, and implement appropriate security measures. Regular communication and collaboration between these teams are essential for addressing emerging cyber threats and ensuring that cost management systems remain secure and resilient. By aligning cost management objectives with IT security priorities, organizations can enhance their cybersecurity posture and protect financial data effectively.

Cyber threats are constantly evolving, requiring organizations to adopt a proactive approach to cybersecurity. Cost managers should implement continuous monitoring mechanisms to detect and respond to potential cyber incidents promptly. This involves deploying intrusion detection systems, security information and event management (SIEM) tools, and endpoint detection and response (EDR) solutions to monitor network traffic and detect suspicious activities. Moreover, organizations should develop comprehensive incident response plans to contain and mitigate the impact of cyber incidents effectively.

In light of the increasing cyber threats facing organizations, cost managers should prioritize investments in cybersecurity technologies and solutions. This includes deploying advanced security tools such as firewalls, antivirus software, and endpoint security platforms to protect against malware and other cyber threats. Additionally, organizations should consider leveraging emerging technologies such as artificial intelligence (AI) and machine learning (ML) to enhance threat detection and response capabilities. By investing in robust cybersecurity technologies, organizations can strengthen their defences and mitigate the risk of costly cyber incidents.

As cost management practices evolve in response to technological advancements and industry trends, cybersecurity will play an increasingly pivotal role in safeguarding financial data and mitigating cyber risks. By integrating cybersecurity into cost management practices, prioritizing data privacy and compliance, investing in cybersecurity training and awareness, collaborating with IT security teams, implementing continuous monitoring and incident response measures, and investing in cybersecurity technologies, organizations can secure the future of cost management and protect their financial assets from cyber threats.

The future of cost management is dynamic and full of possibilities, shaped by emerging technologies, evolving business practices, and shifting market dynamics. In this chapter, we explored various future trends and predictions that will influence the trajectory of cost management in the years to come.

As organizations navigate this ever-changing landscape, it's essential to recognize the importance of staying ahead of the curve and embracing innovation. By leveraging emerging technologies such as artificial intelligence, blockchain, and data analytics, cost managers can unlock new opportunities for efficiency, transparency, and value creation.

Moreover, the integration of sustainability, agile methodologies, and collaborative approaches will redefine the way organizations approach cost management. Embracing a culture of continuous improvement, innovation, and adaptation will be crucial for success in the future of cost management.

Ultimately, the future of cost management holds immense potential for organizations to drive efficiency, resilience, and sustainability in their operations. By embracing emerging trends, fostering collaboration, and prioritizing innovation, organizations can position themselves to thrive in a rapidly changing business environment.

In conclusion, the future of cost management is both challenging and exciting, offering organizations the opportunity to reimagine traditional practices, drive transformative change, and create sustainable value for stakeholders. As we look ahead, it's essential to remain agile, adaptable, and forward-thinking, ready to embrace the opportunities and overcome the challenges that lie ahead in the evolving landscape of cost management.

CHAPTER 11: CONCLUSION

Recap of Key Concepts

As we reach the conclusion of "Mastering Cost Management: Strategies for Effective Project Budgeting and Control," it's essential to revisit the core concepts and methodologies we've explored throughout this journey. These foundational principles form the bedrock of effective cost management and are crucial for achieving project success.

Understanding the Basics of Cost Management

We began by establishing a solid foundation in cost management, defining its scope and importance within project management. Cost management is not just about keeping expenses in check; it's about planning, estimating, budgeting, financing, funding, managing, and controlling costs so that a project can be completed within the approved budget.

Cost Planning: The Blueprint for Success

Cost planning is the initial step that aligns project costs with objectives and overall business goals. It's a proactive approach that involves detailed cost estimation techniques, budgeting, and integrating these plans with the project schedule. Effective cost planning sets the stage for monitoring and controlling costs throughout the project lifecycle.

Techniques for Accurate Cost Estimation

We delved into various cost estimation techniques, from

analogous estimating to more detailed methods like bottom-up and parametric estimating. Each technique has its strengths and applications, depending on the project's complexity and the level of accuracy required. Accurate cost estimation is critical for creating realistic budgets and financial plans.

Cost Control: Keeping Projects on Track

Cost control is the ongoing process of tracking project expenditures and performance against the budget. It involves monitoring cost variances, managing changes, and ensuring that project resources are used efficiently. Tools and techniques like Earned Value Management (EVM) help in quantifying progress and identifying deviations early.

Risk Management in Cost Planning and Control

Identifying and managing cost-related risks is vital for maintaining control over project finances. We explored how to assess and prioritize these risks, develop mitigation strategies, and integrate risk management into both cost planning and control processes. This proactive approach helps in minimizing potential financial impacts on the project.

Value Engineering: Enhancing Project Value

Value engineering is a systematic method to improve the value of a project by optimizing costs and performance. By analysing functions and seeking alternatives, value engineering aims to achieve the best value for money. We discussed the principles, process, and applications of value engineering, demonstrating how it contributes to cost savings and project success.

The Role of Technology in Cost Management

Technological advancements have revolutionized cost management practices. From cost management software solutions to data analytics, Building Information Modelling (BIM), and artificial intelligence, technology offers powerful tools for improving accuracy, efficiency, and decision-making. We examined various technological tools and their integration into cost management processes.

Sustainability and Cost Management

Sustainability is an increasingly critical aspect of cost management. Incorporating sustainable practices not only benefits the environment but can also lead to cost savings. We looked at how to integrate environmental and social costs into project budgeting, achieve savings through sustainable design, and conduct life cycle cost analysis (LCCA) to assess long-term costs and benefits.

Continuous Improvement in Cost Management

The journey of mastering cost management doesn't end with implementing best practices. Continuous improvement is essential for staying ahead in a dynamic business environment. We highlighted the importance of learning from cost overruns and failures, implementing lessons learned, and fostering a culture of continuous improvement. Professional development and leveraging technology also play crucial roles in enhancing cost management practices.

The Future of Cost Management

Finally, we looked towards the future, discussing emerging trends, evolving regulatory standards, and the integration of cost management with other business functions. The future will demand agile and adaptive approaches, the utilization of big data, and new skills and competencies for cost managers.

As we conclude this chapter, it's clear that mastering cost management requires a comprehensive understanding of these key concepts and a commitment to continuous learning and improvement. By integrating these principles into your projects and organizations, you can achieve effective project budgeting and control, leading to greater success and sustainability.

Final Reflections

As we reach the conclusion of "Mastering Cost Management: Strategies for Effective Project Budgeting and Control," it's an opportune moment to reflect on the journey we've undertaken through the pages of this book. The landscape of cost management is ever evolving, driven by advancements in technology, shifts in economic conditions, and the growing emphasis on sustainability and ethical practices. Our goal has been to provide a comprehensive and practical guide that equips you with the knowledge and tools necessary to navigate these changes and excel in your cost management endeavours.

Throughout this book, we've delved into the foundational principles of cost management, explored various methodologies and techniques, and highlighted the importance of integrating cost control with other key project management functions. We've examined the critical role of risk management, the impact of technological advancements, and the necessity of continuous improvement. Each chapter has been crafted to build upon the previous one, creating a cohesive framework that you can apply in your professional practice.

One of the key takeaways from our exploration is the realization that cost management is not a static process. It requires a dynamic and adaptable approach, one that embraces change and leverages innovation. The future of cost management lies in the ability to harness the power of data analytics, artificial intelligence, and other emerging technologies to make informed decisions and optimize resource allocation. As cost managers, it is imperative that we stay abreast of these trends and continuously seek ways to enhance our skills and methodologies.

Another significant aspect we've emphasized is the importance of integrating sustainability into cost management practices. The growing awareness of environmental and social impacts necessitates a shift in how we approach cost planning and control. By adopting sustainable design and construction practices, conducting life cycle cost analyses, and prioritizing sustainable procurement, we can achieve cost savings while contributing to a more sustainable future. This dual focus on cost efficiency and sustainability will become increasingly vital as organizations strive to meet regulatory requirements and societal expectations.

Moreover, the human element of cost management cannot be overlooked. Effective communication, stakeholder engagement, and a culture of continuous improvement are essential components of successful cost management. Building strong relationships with team members, stakeholders, and clients fosters collaboration and ensures that cost management strategies are aligned with broader project and business objectives. Investing in professional development and certification further enhances our ability to lead and innovate in this field.

As we look ahead, the challenges and opportunities in cost management will continue to evolve. The integration of cost management with other business functions, the rise of remote work, and the need for cybersecurity measures are just a few of the trends that will shape the future of this discipline. It is our hope that this book has provided you with a solid foundation and the inspiration to embrace these changes and drive excellence in your cost management practices.

In closing, we extend our deepest gratitude to all who have contributed to this book and to you, our readers, for embarking on this journey with us. May the insights and strategies shared within these pages empower you to master the art of cost management and achieve outstanding results in your projects. The future is full of possibilities, and with the right knowledge and mindset, we can navigate the complexities of cost management with confidence and success.

GLOSSARY OF KEY TERMS

Activity-Based Costing (ABC)

Activity-Based Costing (ABC) is a method of assigning overhead and indirect costs—such as salaries and utilities—to products and services. This system identifies cost drivers and allocates costs based on the actual consumption of each activity, providing a more accurate reflection of the true cost of producing a product or service.

Baseline

A baseline is the original project plan and associated budget, against which actual performance is measured. Establishing a baseline allows project managers to monitor and control project progress and costs, ensuring that deviations are identified and addressed promptly.

Budget

A budget is an estimate of the total cost of completing a project, broken down by task or work package. It serves as a financial plan for project managers to allocate resources efficiently and track expenditures against planned costs.

Cost Control

Cost Control involves monitoring project costs and performance, comparing actual results with the planned budget, and adjusting as necessary to stay within budget. Effective cost control helps ensure that projects are completed within their financial constraints.

Cost Estimation

Cost Estimation is the process of forecasting the financial resources needed to complete a project. It involves determining the quantity and cost of materials, labour, equipment, and other resources required, using various techniques such as expert judgment, analogous estimating, and parametric modelling.

Cost Management Plan

A Cost Management Plan outlines how project costs will be planned, structured, and controlled. It includes details on cost estimation, budgeting, cost control measures, and the methods for reporting and tracking costs throughout the project lifecycle.

Direct Costs

Direct Costs are expenses that can be directly attributed to a specific project or activity, such as labour, materials, and equipment. These costs are easily identifiable and measurable, making them straightforward to allocate to a project.

Earned Value Management (EVM)

Earned Value Management (EVM) is a project management technique used to measure project performance and progress. It integrates scope, time, and cost data to provide a comprehensive view of project status and forecasts future performance based on current trends.

Indirect Costs

Indirect Costs are expenses that cannot be directly linked to a specific project or activity. Examples include administrative overhead, utilities, and facility maintenance. These costs are typically allocated to projects based on a predetermined formula or rate.

Life Cycle Cost Analysis (LCCA)

Life Cycle Cost Analysis (LCCA) evaluates the total cost of ownership of a project or asset over its entire lifespan. It includes initial acquisition costs, operation and maintenance expenses, and disposal costs, providing a comprehensive view of long-term financial implications.

Overhead

Overhead refers to the ongoing administrative expenses not directly tied to a specific project or activity, such as rent, utilities, and executive salaries. These costs are necessary for overall operations but must be allocated across multiple projects or departments.

Parametric Estimating

Parametric Estimating uses statistical relationships between historical data and other variables to predict future costs. This method involves identifying key cost drivers and using mathematical models to estimate project costs based on these variables.

Resource Allocation

Resource Allocation involves distributing available resources —such as personnel, equipment, and budget—across various projects and tasks. Effective resource allocation ensures that projects have the necessary resources to meet their objectives without overextending organizational capacity.

Return on Investment (ROI)

Return on Investment (ROI) is a financial metric used to evaluate the profitability of an investment. It is calculated by dividing the net profit from the investment by the initial cost, providing a percentage that indicates the efficiency of the investment.

Risk Management

Risk Management is the process of identifying, assessing, and mitigating risks that could impact project success. It involves developing strategies to minimize the likelihood and impact of adverse events, ensuring that projects stay on track and within budget.

Scope Creep

Scope Creep refers to the uncontrolled expansion of project scope without corresponding adjustments to time, cost, and resources. It often results from changes or additions to project requirements and can lead to budget overruns and delays.

Total Cost of Ownership (TCO)

Total Cost of Ownership (TCO) includes all costs associated with acquiring, operating, and maintaining a project or asset over its entire lifecycle. TCO provides a comprehensive view of long-term financial commitments, helping organizations make informed investment decisions.

Value Engineering

Value Engineering is a systematic method to improve the value of a project by optimizing its functions. It involves analysing project components and processes to identify cost-saving opportunities without compromising quality or performance.

Work Breakdown Structure (WBS)

A Work Breakdown Structure (WBS) is a hierarchical decomposition of a project into smaller, more manageable components. It breaks down the project scope into deliverables and work packages, providing a framework for planning, estimating, and controlling costs.

Zero-Based Budgeting (ZBB)

Zero-Based Budgeting (ZBB) is a budgeting method where all expenses must be justified for each new period. Unlike traditional budgeting, which adjusts previous budgets, ZBB starts from zero and requires detailed explanations for all proposed costs, promoting efficient resource allocation.

www.ingramcontent.com/pod-product-compliance
Lightning Source LLC
Chambersburg PA
CBHW071917210526
45479CB00002B/455